Dead Serious;

My Life as a Funeral Director

By Kevin Watts

Dead Serious; My Life as a Funeral Director is a memoir. I have tried to recreate events, locales and conversations from my memories of them. In order to maintain their anonymity in some instances I have changed the names of individuals and places, I may have changed some identifying characteristics and details such as physical properties, occupations and places of residence.

Copyright © 2019 by J. Kevin Watts

All rights reserved. Published in the United States of America. No part of this book may be reproduced or transmitted in any form or by any means, graphic, electronic, or mechanical, including photocopying, recording, taping or by any information storage or retrieval system, without the permission in writing from the publisher

ISBN 9798604097809

This book is dedicated to Mr. William J. "Bill" Rogan, who taught me everything I know today about embalming

and to

Mr. Lawrence J. "Larry" Bennett, who taught me to be the very best funeral director that I can

Preface

The funeral profession has always been one of mystique and curiosity. There are many questions asked by those, not in the business regarding how and why we do the things we do.

Some people see us as Ghouls, prospering on the misfortune of those that have suffered a death. Many of us look at ourselves as wanting to help a family that is grieving and making the Funeral or Celebration of life a memorable one, with dignity, respect, and fitting of that person. Many of us work long, tireless hours, days, and weeks. Death has no schedule, nor does it care that it is lunchtime; you are at your child's school play or a holiday.

We are commonly the brunt of many jokes, fables, and wives' tales dating back for years. Since the dawn of man, there has always been one who has had to care for the deceased. Many do not want to deal with it, get their hands dirty or such, but someone must.

The stories, ideas, and ethics expressed in this book are the mortal ramblings of one man who undertook the choice to become that said person. Some refer to him as the Funeral Director, Undertaker or Mortician. Whatever term you wish to describe him, keep in mind. He is a man; He is fallible, and many times he is just like your neighbor or the guy beside you at the supermarket. He is not the creepy older man in black, with cold hands, driving that strange black hearse and talking to you in an eerie manner. Well, Hell, sometimes he is. I've seen that type myself, and frankly he creeps me out!

We aren't all like that

People enter the funeral business for many reasons. Many because it is a family business. Some say they had a "calling" to serve, such as the pastor of a church. Some believe it's all flash and cash, which is not a reason to get into this profession, you will be disappointed! Whatever the reason may be, it is what you make it. If it's not a family business, you almost always "pay your dues" when working your way up the ladder.

Licensure requirements vary by state as to the level of education, length of apprenticeship, etc. In most states, you must register as and serve an apprentice position, and be a graduate of an accredited Mortuary Diploma or Degree Program as required by your area of residency. Many people complete the two concurrently depending on the availability of position and ability to handle both, as it can be difficult.

In 1988, I had completed my time with the US Army and US Coast Guard. Before being discharged from the Coast Guard, I began researching the requirements to become a Funeral Director.

At the time my father-in-law was a retired Brigadier General with the US Air Force and the Air National Guard, a Surgeon and Medical Examiner. He was a significant influence and factor in my career choice. Tom was a remarkable man. He lived fast, on the edge, and everyone joked that he had nine lives. Tom was also a WW II veteran who received two Purple Hearts and a man that I respected and loved.

I lived in Worcester, Massachusetts, in the same condominium complex as my in-laws. My father-in-law would enjoy a cocktail or two at the end of the workday, and by noon on the weekend. Which usually meant that, if available, I was his driver.

Being a driver also meant that I was a secretary, stenographer, photographer, etc. I had grown accustomed to keeping a kit in his trunk so I had everything I might need.

With Massachusetts law allowing Medical Examiners the ability and use of a blue strobe light, much like law enforcement, I had gone out and purchased him one, for our many treks in the night. Although traveling safely and with caution through intersections, it also meant that we went quickly to fatal accidents and crime scenes when needed.

One memorable story that I recall happened back in the late '80s. Tom had called me and asked if I could drive him to a scene. I got up, looked at the clock, noticing that it was around midnight. I went to the restroom, splashed some cold water on my face to wake up, threw on some slacks, a long sleeve shirt and a jacket.
Being November, as it was a crisp New England night but no snow yet that year.

Once we met downstairs in the parking lot, I grabbed my kit from the trunk which included the blue strobe light, placed it on the dash at which point he said that we would not need that. I acknowledged, put it back into my case in the trunk and climbed back into the driver's seat. I had asked if we were not going to a crime scene. He stated that we were merely making a House Call. I did not pursue the matter anymore, as it wasn't uncommon for Tom to perform a House Call to one of his buddies or patients in the middle of the night, as had been a common practice from time to time. I will say this, Tom was a different doctor if you needed medical attention

after hours and on the weekend. If he knew you, he was there to help you.

After being notified of the address, I quickly made our way there. The location was one of the more affluent areas in Worcester. Larger estate-style homes, all with gated driveways. Upon reaching the address, Tom removed a piece of paper from his pocket. He read to me what the gate code was. I entered it, and the gate slowly opened. As we pulled forward the gate closed, I climbed the long winding driveway, parking to the outside of the circular drive in front of the house.

As Tom began to exit, I did as well to grab his medical kit from the trunk. He informed me that this was a house call, but that the patient was nervous and uneasy with people they were unfamiliar with. He stated that it might be best if I remained in the car. At first, I was well, ok, but I obliged, thinking I would sit, listen to the radio and catch a nap.

After about twenty minutes, there was a knock on the driver's side window. Startled, I turned to find a gentleman standing in a robe holding a large platter. As I rolled down the window, he stated that the homeowner thought I might like something to eat and drink. I thanked him for his hospitality, accepted and pulled in the tray, rolling up the window as the man walked away, up the stairs back into the home. I thought that was a little weird, but I was happy about the thought.

There was just about anything that you could want: fruit, cheese, crackers, soft drinks, and water. I placed the platter on the dash, nibbled for a bit and eventually nodded off into a nap. After a long day and a full tummy, I would not last long at 1 AM.

I heard the passenger door open, and I jumped as I awoke. Tom had tossed his medical kit onto the seat. As I yawned, stretched and exited the car, I grabbed the case, returning it to the trunk. I noticed that the clock in the car read 4:30 AM. I asked what I should do with the platter and he said to take it and place it on the front porch. I did, and we exited the property, with the gate automatically opening as we approached it to leave.

I noticed that Tom's white dress shirt had blood splatters on it and the sleeves, which were rolled up. I wanted to ask, but knowing Tom, you didn't. There would be a more appropriate time to question the events of that night. We were both tired, needed to get home, and that was not the moment.

Weeks later, after researching who lived at that address, I found out it was someone who had attended my wedding and was a longtime childhood friend of Tom's. In my mind, I think this is a scene right out of a crime/drama movie, of which I was entirely correct.

Later, Tom would confide in me that the gentleman in question, whose residence we were at, had several employees. One of which had been shot and could not go to the hospital. They require gunshot wounds to be reported to the authorities. You don't just go running off to the hospital with a gunshot wound without expecting a barrage of questioning. It's best to know someone on the professional level who can take care of said things privately for you. I've even seen occasionally a few RNs that were just as able to remove and dress a bullet wound, but that is entirely another chapter.

One of the best pieces of advice that Tom ever conveyed to me over the years is "the most important thing in this world is Friends." Every so often, something may come up, and you might need a favor. You perform a favor, you receive a favor, but that is how the world turns. To this day, I've always remembered and lived by that statement.

When the Fall of 1988 rolled around, I began classes at the local Mortuary College in Boston. The school later merged with Mount Ida College in Newton, MA. I received my Associate from Mount Ida, later transferring credits and graduating from Boston University. I was a high school drop-out, who foolishly left, half-way through my senior year. I thought work and money were more important than education. When it was all said and done, I finished with a 3.8-grade point average. I was happy to have made such an accomplishment and my mother jokingly smacked me up aside my head and asked "Why didn't you do that well in High School?"

For three years, I made that dreaded drive down the Massachusetts Turnpike, US-93, and Storrow Drive to and from class. I worked my way through college, much as I did in high school, in construction, banging nails, framing houses, general carpentry, demolition, etc. I was fortunate enough to have an employer that let me start early and leave in time to make the drive to Boston to attend classes.

After hanging off the side of a house in the cold New England, frigid temperatures, in the middle of winter, or the heat of the Summer, an hour ride in the heat or air conditioning for an hour to Boston was a welcome relief at the end of a workday, four days a week.

After the second semester, I found an apprenticeship with a Funeral Home in Worcester. That was a lifesaver because, in one class, my grades were suffering. It dealt with a lot of terminology about different services, churches, faiths, etc. Many times I did not understand what they were speaking of. When I began my apprenticeship, it all fell into place. Years ago, families went to a particular Funeral Home because there was a history of serving that family in the past.

The Funeral Home that I worked at until 1991 was one of the larger Irish Catholic Funeral Homes in Worcester. Our clientele was probably about 90 percent Irish Catholic families. The remaining 10 percent were Protestant, Armenian, Orthodox Greek, and Italian Catholic.

I enjoyed the funeral home that I worked in, and I have some very fond memories of my employers and the staff. The owner and his son were great guys, letting me grab all the hours that I could. They were very understanding about my educational schedule and that I had a family to feed. There was another gentleman who merged his business into theirs and was a very knowledgeable man. He was always a prankster, and I think that is why we worked so well together, and the embalmer, who had a good sense of humor himself.

The embalmer Bill was a unique individual, and I enjoyed working with him immensely. He was an Army veteran of WW II, serving in the Company A 749th Tank Battalion alongside his twin brother. They both saw front line combat in Normandy, Northern France, Rhineland, and Central Europe. He was also a purple heart recipient. Bill always took the time to answer questions and to explain things. He explained to me that there are many reasons we take great care to perform our duties in the preparation room, and many reasons things we see, hear, say or do, never leave the back room. And that has always stuck with me for years. Confidentiality is key to keeping the interest and privacy of the families we serve paramount. I may talk about experiences during my life as a funeral director, but I have kept specific details vague, to protect identities of the clients and their families I have served over the years.

One thing to keep in mind in the funeral profession is always to have an open mind. There is still room to learn, grow, and adapt. You can ask ten different Embalmers to perform the same task, and you may see ten different methods, all productive and efficient. If you walk into any situation with an open mind, you will learn a lot. I have always enjoyed talking to "old Timers" in the trades. Both funeral directors and embalmers. I appreciate what they share, from a different era, not having some technology that we have today.

Over time I have noticed and stated to this day is how embalming technology has changed over the years. You can watch someone embalm, what vessels they use, habits, mannerisms, and almost tell what year they went to Mortuary College or the era that their embalming instructor attended whether it be the Axillary Artery the Femoral or the Carotid. People ask me what my preferred artery of injection is, I always reply, the Popliteal. Which is a joke because its location is behind the kneecap and difficult to access.

Worcester, Massachusetts is commonly referred to as the City of Three-Deckers. Three-deckers were about the footprint of a single-story home, mostly of 2-3 bedrooms. The only difference is these were three levels, sometimes that third level being 20-30 feet in height.

Daniel Hall, a journalist, writing in 1947 for the Worcester Telegram characterized the city's three-deckers as "monuments to a time of good workmanship, good family life, and good practical answers to the problem of rapid city expansion." They were built throughout the second half of the nineteenth century and into the twentieth century to provide inexpensive housing to the waves of immigrants arriving in Worcester each year to work in the factories.

Many families lived in three-deckers, and with my era of apprenticeship being in the '80s, home visitations were common practice back then.

We would have a 200 lb male or female, embalmed, dressed, laid out in a lovely red cherry finish, half-couch casket, wrapped with a padded mover's blanket, two guys up above pulling, an apprentice (usually me) below, pushing that casket upwards three flights of stairs, to its destination. Trust me, I was in much better shape back then, but I did it. The combined weight of both casket and a person could easily be 350 - 450 pounds.

I cringed every time I heard those words uttered that the family wants a home visitation, as all I could think about was "Oh God, not another three-decker." But, every few instances, on a rare occurrence, we only had to go to the first or second level. Some days my hands would be bruised and beaten worse maneuvering a casket containing a person up the three flights of stairs, than a hard day at my construction job.

Other memories include the fact that we had the agreement to handle all deaths and funerals at the Sisters of Notre Dame. It was a large facility, filled with retired nuns who had living quarters on the premises. If at any point any of the sisters got to where they needed a nursing home type environment or care, they had a wing/facility for that. Most of the nuns were great people. They were always upbeat, cheery, and friendly.

When one nun passed away, they would call us to handle the funeral arrangements. Bill and I would perform the embalming, dressing and later casket them, and we would work the funeral with the director. We would place the departed nun in the chapel on grounds at the facility one evening the night before the funeral mass the next morning. The family of the nun was usually the ones coordinating the day and time of the service, based around their availability to travel, etc.

Back in the day, when I first began my apprenticeship, we could not take the nuns back to the funeral home for the embalming. We would have to transport our equipment to the facility, and they had a room set up for us to perform the embalming, accompanied by another sister or two. During that time we had to transport our embalming machine, a portable embalming table, usually made of stainless steel, many instruments, glass jars, and hoses to collect the fluids. Then, several hours later, after we had completed the embalming and the area we used, cleaned, we would transfer everything back to the Funeral Home, and all the blood/body fluids disposed of accordingly.

I would occasionally hear the story about not having the modern marvels of an electric embalming machine and aspirator, and the horror stories of how everything used to be. Having to use a bulb type device that would be manually pumped as you squeezed it in your hand. Along with the use of gravity feed bottles to inject embalming fluid into the body while blood drained downward by hose into a collection jar on the floor.

Usually, the gravity feed bottle, attached to a tall ladder, higher than the body. I always remember the statement back in class and equate it to this very situation. For every foot above the body, the gravity feed bottle is, you usually get a half-pound of pressure. So, if you were looking for 6 pounds of pressure, of the fluid going into the body, you had better be 12 feet higher than the body with your feed bottle. Ha, like anyone has ceilings that high! Which usually meant you would be there a while.

They later allowed us to transfer the departed Sisters to the Funeral Home on each instance to perform our duties. It worked out very well for all of us. We had more time to do a more thorough job for the best optimum results.

Now, not only did the sisters have a place to live and nursing facilities on the property. They also had their Cemetery, where most of the nuns would be interred after the funeral mass. Some would retire back to their cities of origin and buried in a family plot. But, I think most of them considered that they had given their lifetime duties and purpose to serve the Lord, so most just thought it was fitting to be buried in the Cemetery on grounds at Notre Dame. And there was no cost for the family of the sister to do so.

The only problem was that the caretaker of the cemetery did not have the means to open a grave after the ground had frozen. Depending on the area, in the New England region, it is not uncommon to have a 24–30-inch deep frost lines. The only method to make the ground soft enough to dig is with the use of a ground warmer or defroster. A ground warmer is placed on top of, or partially sunken into the ground and looks like a rusted oblong tank or barrel. It is like the upper half of a barbecue smoker. There is usually a three-inch hole at one end, through which you place a burner. The burner is essentially a roofer's torch connected to a propane tank. The burner emits a flame and heat used to thaw the ground with the help of the ground warmer.

Its typical placement is on the grave 24 hours before digging the grave so that the heat will thaw the area. I believe the general rule was that it would melt at 1 inch per hour, depending on the environment. And, you have better make sure you had enough propane for the task at hand. Whether thawing a grave or grilling, no one wants to run out of propane.

Sisters of Notre Dame had a deal worked out with the local Catholic cemetery. If the weather conditions were not permissible to open the grave for a burial, we would have the interment ceremony in the Narthex of the convents' chapel, after the funeral mass. I would later drive over to the Catholic cemetery, the grounds crew would meet me, and they would inter the Sister into a Mausoleum. Then, in the spring, the caretaker could accommodate for the graves to be dug. During those winter months, this could be merely three graves that needed to be dug at first opportunity to do so, to lay the departed nuns to rest. Or, this could be 8–10 graves that needed to be opened and prepared. I remember two spring days, all I did was shuttle about ten sisters from the mausoleum, back to the cemetery at Notre Dame in our Hearse.

Yes, with me being the curious one, I felt the urge to crack open the casket and sneak a peek. Not much had changed. Most were just as beautiful and pristine as the day we had the funeral. Again, our embalmer took the time to teach me about preservation customs and to do things in a particular manner, for best results. I wished that he was still alive, just so I could say thank you, one last time.

Back to apprenticeship duties, which meant you did every job at the funeral home, which included cleaning everyone's mess, the bathrooms, vacuuming, painting, cleaning windows and in my case, I even performed construction projects around the place, just because I knew how to. Duties of which would also include washing and detailing the hearse and station wagon we used for flowers.

If you've ever washed a car in the cold, frigid New England winter, then you know of what I am speaking. So cold, it takes about 15 minutes in the heat, for your hands to warm up and for the throbbing of pins and needles to leave your fingers. The trouble is, this was to take place before each funeral. On a particular morning, I was to wash the hearse. Afterward, I was to load the casket, and we were all to meet at the church. The family was not coming to the funeral home the morning of the funeral mass.

I was late to the funeral home. I had not allowed myself enough time to get the hearse washed and prepared for the funeral that morning. I figured no problem. I would make a mad dash down to the car wash and run through before I had to be at the church. Simple enough. Occasionally I had been told that we never take the hearse through the car wash, unless it was an absolute emergency, as the owner wanted to keep the finish in pristine condition. With me being the person who washes and waxes the vehicles, I can understand that way of thinking. But it should be clean for this person's funeral, and I thought this would represent an emergency.

The rational part of me also considered it might be worse to take the hearse through the car wash, with a casket in the back. So, I made my way to the garage and grabbed the quilted cover that we use, mostly when we transport the casket into a home, for home visitations. After I shook it out and placed it over the casket, concealing it from the clear view of the window of the rear door, I was off. I turned onto the street and pulled into the car wash. I paid the guy cash, as to not use the coupons in the glove compartment. Oh, how I thought I was slick. This would work out just fine. There would still be enough time for them to dry the car and for me to be at the church for my scheduled arrival time. As the guy motioned me forward onto the tracks, I removed my hands from the wheel and placed the car into neutral. As I felt the forward movement of the hearse, I knew it was on its way to being clean and pristine for the funeral.

 First came the spraying of water and suds onto the finish in a pre-soak fashion, then I could see the soapy suds covering the hood and windshield. Then came a sound that I will never forget until the day I die. A racket at which point my heart sank to the fathoms I thought I would never see it again. A loud pop, followed by a horn siren that would emit a beep that lasted about a second, followed by a second of silence. The siren would keep repeating and was load as Hell. Everything was running. The siren was continuing to beep as the hearse was standing still. I said to myself, "Oh Shit!"

My first thought was that the hearse had jumped off the track. Now, the problem with that in my mind is that if one car jumps the track, another car behind could be pushed into your vehicle. Or, being off the track means you could hit equipment on either side of the car. Meaning scratches, dents or other damage to an $80,000 vehicle. The bad part of this scenario is that I have a Funeral to get to and a casket in the back of the hearse. Not an ideal situation for anyone.

After the technician could turn off the horn and shut down the machinery and wash cycle, they came out to check on me. I rolled down the window, soap suds all inside the car and all over me. They explained to me that the track system had broken. Without the track system to project the vehicle to the exit of the car wash, I was stuck. I thought, No Problem, drive right out. Well, not that simple. The track remnants were in my way that had to be removed. Without their removal, I had no path for the tires to travel, so I could not get out. As I checked my watch, waiting for them to clear a path, I worried that I would be late to the church. As soon as they gave me the thumbs up, I exited the car wash, pulled to the side, and exited the car, so I could make sure there was no damage to the hearse. There was not, and the guys helped me do a quick hand wash and dry on the car.

As I prayed and talked to the big man upstairs, I made my way to the church. Please, Lord let me make it there. I promise I'll always allow myself time and never be late again; I promise!

My mind raced a hundred miles an hour, as did my heart. What excuse could I possibly give for being late? I pulled in front of the church 15 minutes late and given the look of disapproval from my boss, as I thought to myself, "Here it comes." As I exited, I appeared upset, complaining about traffic, traffic lights, etc. Grumble, grumble, grumble.

I grabbed the church truck and bounded up the granite stairs to the entry of the church, placing it in position. We all grabbed the casket, carried it up the steep stairs, placed in on the truck, and moved it to the side of the Narthex. After I had closed the hearse door and returned to take my place inside near the casket, the front door of the church opened, and the family entered. I grabbed keys, parked and lined up the family cars for the procession and thanked my lucky stars that everything worked out that day.

It was a valuable lesson learned. Several, honestly, place nothing off until the last minute. Never take the hearse through the car wash. And never, under any circumstances have a casket in the hearse, when taking it through a car wash.

3.

It is always great to know others in college in the same classes. I was a wiz with embalming, chemistry, English; I just sucked at math. So, it's good to have some study mates to compare notes. The friendships you make today will lead to expressed friendships in life. Back in New England, I usually made it a practice to ask classmates for help if I needed it in their areas and often offered it in mine. This proved true with death certificates and burial permits, which were filed on a town level. Not according to county and state, like many health departments do today.

We would work funerals for a classmate's family firm. Sometimes you need to rent a hearse for a funeral. Sometimes you need someone to embalm and are in a jam. That's how we rolled back in school. And, a lot of that has followed and will follow that generation. I will have to say, I have seen some nasty people in this profession, but I have seen some good-hearted souls and legends.

There was a group of about seven of us that clicked and became close friends, and we shared many fun times. Whether it be a drink after a long four nights of class, after a week of employment full time, etc., we were all together.

Once I bought one of those Halloween decorations, which comprised an arm inside of a shirt sleeve with a rubber hand. I bought it months prior and finally found an opportunity to use it. A member of our group would have to hit Logan Airport on a specific night, after class to pick up a body that was flying in.

Each course was weekly and usually began with a test at the start of every class. We would usually park in the library parking lot, which was where we gathered to meet and do a group study.

I located the hearse belonging to Alex's family-owned funeral home, parked far away, as to not draw the attention of classmates or the public. He had to make that pick-up at 10 PM. His father had no one else available to go, and it was convenient for Alex to go right after class.

I looked around to make sure no one was watching me as I checked to see if the rear cargo door was unlocked. I looked like a kid on

Christmas Morning! Many hearses during that era have an issue with the cargo door and the ability to lock with the key fob. You would usually have to lock the door manually with the key and sometimes people might forget to do so. I slowly opened the door and wedged the soft, padded portion deeply below the lower door hinge, slowly closing and applying weight, as to be ever so quiet closing it. There it was. An arm was hanging out of the back of a hearse, appearing to dangle as it made its way down the road.

I returned to the library, met the others, studied, chatted, and made our way to class. It was a usual night. A test, a returned test from last week, more notes and dismissal. We all departed and made our way to our cars. It was the following evening when I received that call. Alex's dad was pissed. I'm talking worse than pissed. He was super pissed! He had many calls from people on Storrow Drive and US 93 on his way home.

He was talking so fast. I can't count how many complaints he received by phone. His dad finally accepted the fact that it was a College Prank, which it was, and let it go. We had a ton of laughs in college. It was but one of many goofs that we all had pulled on each other as friends. Which seemed to strengthen our bond together, making several years go quickly, yet too fast.

Another prank that stands out in the Greats of the Greats category is the Mob Letter prank. This came to mind after the previous house call story. One kid in our class was actively an embalmer apprentice, getting his license as both funeral director and embalmer, but working in the capacity as embalmer on most days.

Lee worked for Sam and her husband. Sam had married into her husband's family business and had to get her license to take part in the company dealings. Lee and Sam would commute together regularly from Cranston, RI to Boston to save gas and wear on a vehicle. We were friends with both Sam and Lee and they were part of our group.

Now Lee had worked in an area, not too far from a less than a desirable part of Providence, RI. They embalmed at this facility and would ship out to several other locations for visitations and Funerals once they had prepared the deceased individual. One day there was a shooting outside of the building. It occurred on the back porch stairway leading to an apartment over the funeral home. There was a teen that lived over the funeral home with his mother. They watched the place at night and on weekends and it somehow involved him in the shooting. Lee had overheard a conversation with the teen resident and the victim prior to the shooting.

I don't know all the details other than Lee, and his supervisor audibly heard the conversation through the wall, heard the shotgun blast afterward and called the PD after witnessing the person fleeing and the body on the stairwell.

Lee sat out of class the next day. We talked to Sam, who confirmed the story. She told us after a day or two, he would come back to classes.

It was during this time, our friend Jake and I thought we would cheer Lee up and make him laugh. Knowing the details of the shooting, we schemed a note that we would write to Lee. In the letter, we informed him we knew that he was a witness, that we knew he had talked to the Police and that we would exact our revenge on him.

Now, you would have to have known Jake and I to understand the humor in this. We were the pranksters in our group We were to trim out different sized letters from a magazine and compose the letter conveying our message to him. Assemble it onto a blank piece of paper, with a glue stick and tweezers, like they do on television and pop it in the mail to him.

After the day we were confident that the letter would arrive, we kept in close contact, asking each other for info. Finally, when we least expected it Sam walked into the library, with a horrific look, telling us about Lee, the letter, the local PD was actively searching for whoever sent that letter.

When we heard that, we looked at each other with literally the same "Oh Shit" look in our eyes. But we had mailed it in Providence; It had a Providence postmark on it, and we knew they could not tie it to us. Although it took a ton of convincing him it was, in fact, Jake and I that sent the letter. It also took a lot of expressing our heartfelt apologies, that we were genuinely sorry and begging for forgiveness. We didn't intend to scare him and it probably wasn't in our best judgment to have pulled the prank.

Afterward, all seven of us laughed and laughed, thinking back in retrospect. Lee even laughed saying he made his wife walk down the driveway to check the mail each day, and how he wouldn't as much as leave the house to go to the supermarket.

Attending college in Boston near Fenway Park had its perks. We skipped class and caught many Red Sox games, whether it be in person or having a beer and watching the game at the pubs. I caught some of the best punk and rock shows at some excellent venues. Bunratty's, Channel and the Rat were some of my old stomping grounds, and it was a different time back then.

When graduation rolled around, we all saw each other less. Then less became never. Many times I've thought about everyone. I wonder how and where they are now. I heard that one classmate had walked away from a family business to pursue his own dreams. I guess you get caught up in life, family, and career and wonder where the time goes.

Immediately after graduation, I had taken the National Board Exam for Funeral Service, followed by the Massachusetts State Board Exam. Boom! I was a Licensed Funeral Director, Baby!

Which wasn't much of advancement above apprentice, other than you had a license to perform additional duties. If you had proven your mettle, your tenacity, and your ability to do everything the way your employer wanted it done, then they would place faith in you to do so.

After graduation and securing licensure, I faced a tough decision. I left my employer in Worcester to move 106 Miles southeast back to Cape Cod. I frowned upon leaving a firm that had employed me, put up with my educational schedule and availability. It is not really in good taste to do so, but I had to decide. The Cape seemed like a better place to raise a family, better schools without having to go to private schools, and the real estate market seemed keen for both buyers and sellers. We looked and found a great buildable lot, right across from the local elementary school.

Upon moving back to the Cape, I quickly began making the rounds. I threw on my best suit, a stylish tie, and the sharply starched white dress shirt. A shirt starched and pressed in such a fashion that if I turned my head too quickly, I thought might slash my throat. With resumes in hand, I began my excursion. I traveled to all 15 towns on the Cape and called on all 14 Funeral Homes. No one was hiring. I ventured beyond the Cape. I hit Funeral Homes beyond that radius. I hit any business that I could, to no avail. Finally, I found a job with a casket company out of Providence that needed a salesman. I didn't want a sales job, commission, and miles on my car, but I had no choice. I had to go where the money was, and my family needed to eat.

I was happy to have a job; Although I didn't care much for sales, I was good at it. The pricing was right for the caskets I was selling, and I had the support of the company. Occasionally, they would ask me to accept deliveries and deliver at night to some funeral homes. Somehow I got the feeling that these caskets may be warm to the touch and had fallen off of the back of a truck.

One evening I was driving to Boston from Providence to make a delivery I had an 18 gauge steel protective casket and a child's casket in the back of the van. As I exited 95 North, I had to jockey for a position to enter I-93. As I swerved, the child's casket overturned. When I reached my destination, I backed to the designated garage door and waited for the person meeting me to return with a cart to unload both caskets.

I opened the rear to the van and reached to upright the small casket. As I did, I noticed that the lid had opened and something had fallen out. As I rolled the casket to its original position, that's when I saw it. It was cash. It was a stack of hundreds, bundled with a paper band around it and it had fallen out onto the floor. My eyes grew, my jaw dropped, I heard the guy returning, and I quickly shoved it back inside. In doing so is when I saw the other bundles of cash inside. I quickly closed the casket. Once he reached the van, we unloaded both caskets. I had him sign for both, and I was about to leave when he suggested that I accompany him down to the corner for a beer. I tried to get out of it as it was late and I still had to return the van to Providence and drive back to the Cape.

After a few more requests, I gave in and said that I would have one beer. I usually wouldn't have, but this guy was close friends with the owner of the casket company. After I parked the van in his funeral home lot, we made the walk several blocks away to Triple O's Lounge. He greeted and said hello to several of his friends. After a few beers, I stated that I needed to make my trek back home. That's when I knew that I needed to make my way on to another employer. I wasn't sure what was up with the casket company, but I knew that it was something that I didn't need to be in the middle of.

I always kept my ear to the ground in case I heard of anyone needing a funeral director or embalmer. I felt that it was in my best interest to get away from that situation as quickly as possible.

In my casket sales travels, I called upon a funeral home in Marstons Mills, Massachusetts one day. I met a great guy that day who was one of two business partners that started that funeral home in 1983. "Jack" gave me a tour of the funeral home, part of which was an old schoolhouse from the 1800s. We talked about their business, my move to Cape Cod and how he might work me into a part-time position of making removals, embalming and such. It worked out to be a great stepping stone for me to find work. Sadly, Jack passed away several months after that because of health issues. I honestly wished that I had gotten to know him better, but I am grateful for the time that I had with him.

Jack's business partner, Larry, was a great guy. I value the time that we spent and worked together, which was almost 15 years. Larry was funny, a hard-working man who was deeply devout to his family, religion, the community, and until the day he sold the funeral home, ran it according to the dream and customs that he and Jack had envisioned, practiced and shared.

I will always hold Larry near and dear to my heart as the epitome of a mentor, teacher, and friend. We butted heads several times, on specific issues, and I feel we learned from each other. One admirable thing that I can always say about Larry is that he was not only fair, but he also was generous as an employer. He always respected his employees and that they make time to spend with their family, which is a hard thing to juggle in the funeral profession. I also remember Larry working with families that might have a hardship issue. They may not have always been able to afford what they wished, but he went to great lengths to help if he could.

In the beginning, my work at the funeral home in Marstons Mills was primarily picking up the deceased individuals, or "removals" as we commonly refer them to in the business, and embalmings.

Hell, I was happy to have work and to be getting paid at this point. The funeral home in Marstons Mills had a spacious prep room. The prep room is the area where an individual is embalmed and held until we dress them, the cosmetics applied, and placed into the casket, before their viewing or services. It was standard in that it had one embalming machine, one embalming table, and a dressing table. With plenty of working room, two or even three employees could all perform separate tasks, at the same time preparing for impending wakes, services, etc.

Unlike Worcester, where I worked for a primarily Irish Catholic funeral home, that had a rather small volume of work that was cremation and maybe 10% services at Protestant churches. The Cape was an abundance of different faiths and customs of which I enjoyed being a part of.

We worked at many of the Catholic churches, an array of Protestant Churches, and the Quaker meetinghouses, Episcopal, Baptist, Orthodox Jewish, and merely funerals in the funeral home. One thing about the Cape people migrated there from many places in the state, and the country, over the years, and it reflects that in their religious and personal customs.

First Calls in the funeral business are the first contact that you have with a family member, nurse, social worker or anyone who may call you from an institution, alerting you that there has been a death and that they are ready for you to make your way to their destination for the removal.

When taking the first call, you try to gather as much info as possible. It is helpful to know what circumstances you are dealing with before arrival. You want to gather as much info as possible, but you do not want to upset the caller either. Most of the time, a caller, especially a family member, can have a vast amount of emotions flowing, heightened sensitivity, etc.

Most of the time, if it's a hospice nurse calling, they will advise you of any circumstances of which they should make you aware. For example, weight, stairs, a large family on-site, to call upon arrival as it is a gated community, etc. Most hospice nurses that I have ever met are invaluable to their profession and to the families they serve.

It takes an extraordinary person to put up with some families I have encountered in almost 30 years.

Memories of one particular hospice nurse stand out from over the years. Most times, we have to subscribe to strict protocols and practices in our professional life, primarily when it deals with the privacy of patients. But, the result is that we as health care professionals, or in our case, death care professionals, all want to remain safe and go home to our families at the end of a sometimes long day.

After receiving the first call from the nurse, that we had a removal, at said location and that this was a hospice passing within the confines of a residential address, we got ready to depart.

It always rang out in my mind as if we were firefighters, donning our gear, ready to roll out into the world, unsure of what we may encounter. We typically wore blue jeans and a button-down dress shirt or golf shirt to work, as we were usually doing anything from maintenance, cleaning, clerical. Running errands and cleaning cars to prepare for a forthcoming funeral.

Now, you have two guys quickly donning suits and ties, getting a stretcher into the station wagon or van to be on their way as soon as possible. A stretcher, or cot, is the common term given to the wheeled apparatus that funeral homes used to transport a deceased individual. Yes, the old joke is "they're not going anywhere," but you don't want the family to wait a long time for your arrival. And, when there is a death, it can seem like an eternity for those waiting for your arrival.

As one guy loaded the stretcher into the car to pull around back and pick the other up, the other individual usually checked the files to see if the person in question had any pre-arrangements in place. Pre-arrangements, just as they infer, are advance directives, sometimes paid in full, what the person may have selected, and even purchased before the need has arisen. It helps upon arrival when you talk to the family members, so they are not inundated with questions that they shouldn't be.

When dispatched, they informed us that no next of kin was on the scene, just the nurse. Upon arrival, we exchanged introductions, made small talk about the weather, etc. As the nurse led us over, we approached and noticed the gentleman lying in a hospital bed in the middle of the living room, which can be the norm. Many of these beds can be large, cumbersome, and difficult to move into bedrooms in homes.

As we began to position and readied the stretcher, she whispered: "You will want to practice universal precautions." I looked at her, kept getting the stretcher ready, and I asked: "Ok, what are we talking here?"

Again, she looked at me and stated: "You will want to practice universal precautions" Again, I asked her What was the patient's medical history, etc. that would lead her to say that.

Upon the third time, she stated that we would want to practice universal precautions; I began to put everything back onto, tidy up the stretcher and motioned to my co-worker that we would be leaving. Abruptly, she stated, "What are you doing?" I then instructed her we are leaving. If you want to play this game, speaking in riddles and not be upfront with us, we're leaving. It's that simple.

She then got testy and short with her answers, told me that the gentleman had AIDS, and was I happy now. I said, No. Now, I am satisfied that you are leveling with me. I also stated that we are all in a collective effort to serve the families and the individual. If I should go back to the funeral home, perform the embalming, stick myself with an instrument or a needle, that I damn well deserve to know what the medical history is. It was none of my business about the gentleman's personal history, private life, or lifestyle choices. But if there is something I should know for my sake or the sake of my coworkers or family, then I deserve to know.

Everything seemed to cool down after that. We gathered our paperwork made our way out to our vehicle and departed for the funeral home. Upon returning, I had a note on my desk to call the hospice organization. I did, and I spoke to a supervisor there, who wanted to give me the same old song and dance as the hospice nurse about patient confidentiality. And, I again gave the same speech, that they can do whatever they choose, but they need to have the professional courtesy to communicate the facts and necessities to one another so we are all on the same page.

There are too many instances where things can go wrong because of a lack of or a breakdown in communication. Our job is to be there and perform our duties to the best of our ability for the families we serve. If you compromise in certain areas, it shows. If a family has a better experience because a funeral director understood the circumstances and helped that family, considering the tone and elements, then I say Job well done. But, in all actuality, we all have a right to know the patient's medical history.

6.

Getting back to removals, you never really know what to expect until you arrive. It could be anything from the mundane to the unusual. The circumstances in which people die and are found can be surprising. Just like when your grandmother used to tell you, "Be sure that you are wearing clean underwear. You never know when you might get hit by a bus." My catchy reply was, "Well, if I see the bus approaching, they will be soiled anyway!"

But her meaning was understood and appreciated when I began seeing the compromising positions people could be found in at death. Some clothed, some not! I will list a few of the removals that have hung in my limited memory over the years. I may ramble, so please keep up.

Many times a relative might not reach a person by phone for an extended period. Often they will call the local police or sheriff's department and ask them to do a "Welfare Check." Which is as it sounds. Can you please stop by and check on Dad, his wellbeing or welfare, as we live out of town.

And, many times, that is how someone is found, deceased at home. Afterward, usually, the Medical Examiner or Coroner backtracks a timeline, when the last contact someone had with the individual circumstances in which found, etc.

It was a sunny, Summer evening when we received such a call to pick up a gentleman at home. We would refer to an unattended death when the police were on the scene as a police call. So, we all knew not to dillydally, get there, and pick up the individual so they could clear the scene. Sometimes there were family members on location; sometimes there were not. In this specific scene, and some others, it was probably best that there was not.

From the first appearance, the gentleman who was deceased was sitting at his dining room table, nude, paying bills, writing checks, and getting them ready to mail. He had a heart attack, had fallen out of the chair, into the floor, right hand over his chest, lying face down on the carpet. As we rolled him over to straighten out his arms and legs, to get him onto the stretcher, I moved his left arm. I noted the paper he clenched in his left hand. It took several minutes to unclench his fist and remove the crumpled paper. When I did and saw the phone company logo across the top, I said: "Damn that had to be one Hell of a Phone Bill!"

Everyone chuckled, appreciated the levity, but then it was back to business, gather the info we needed to track down the Doctor to sign the death certificate and make our way back to the funeral home.

Every so often, you will run across a decomp case. A decomp case refers to someone who has died, been there for an extended period, and decomposition has occurred. Once the body dies, decay begins. Certain factors will cause someone to decompose rapidly and specific factors that will slow down the process.

This decomp case in question was when I was an apprentice and lived in Worcester, MA. We were short-handed, told the dispatcher that I could come, but would be by myself. He stated that it was ok that one officer could assist. Once there, I was instructed to go to the steps and up to the third story of a three-decker. As soon as I exited the car, I could smell the horrid stench that invaded my nostrils. As I made my way upstairs, it got worse. Once through the front door, I was waived to the bathroom where, in the tub, I found a murky, grey, nasty bathtub full of human stew. If there was ever a day that would make someone question their career choice, it was that day, my friend.

I could feel the gag reflex kicking in. I held it back, and I kept telling myself that it would all be over soon. You need to get through this; I repeated over in my mind. I carefully thought in my head how I would get the body out of the tub. I carefully thought about how I would get her out of the Goo. And how I would get her onto my stretcher. I went back down to the hearse. Yes, we used a hearse for removals back in the late '80s at this funeral home.

I grabbed a bottle of vicks we kept in the glove compartment for just such instances, a pouch or body bag to contain the remains and several pairs of gloves. As I returned to the third floor, I removed my jacket, tie, rolled up my sleeves, and went to the kitchen. Once there, I located a box of garbage bags and returned to the bathroom. Gloves were too short, so I donned a garbage bag on each arm. I had one officer pull and tie the drawstrings together, behind my back. I opened the pouch onto the floor by the tub, and with one hand I raked the muck from the drain and the other I began to pick out flesh and bone, chucking it into the pouch. It took all of an hour to get the tub drained and every bit out and into the body bag.

As I got ready to leave and had gathered everything to dispose of back at the funeral home, one cop helped me get the stretcher down to and into the hearse. He commented to me, "You earned your money today." My response if I remember correctly was "No Shit" or something quick and to the point. He laughed. I didn't.

That was one of the longest rides I have ever taken. The stench had almost embedded itself into my nostrils. I could only imagine how bad it was into the interior of our Caddy Hearse. Less than two miles away from the funeral home, I hear sirens and see blue lights behind me. I was being pulled over by the police. Had I forgotten something? Had I been speeding? I was unsure.

As the officer made his way from his car up to the window, I watched as he got right up on my window, he began by saying "I pulled you over because you were speeding." As he continued, the look on his face went pale. He began swatting the air in front of his face. He then began spewing a list of profanities. Most of which I could only make out was "Good God! What in the F' is that smell? What is that? Holy Shit!"

Yadda, yadda, yadda. I explained that I had been down at Elm Street on an unattended death call. I was on my way to the medical examiner's office with the remains. The stench overcame me. I was just as unhappy as he was. It would probably take weeks to get the smell out of me and the car. If he didn't believe me, he could call dispatch to verify.

His words were, "Go! Go! Get the F' out of here. I'm getting sick! Just go!" I laughed a little. I was mad that this unholy Hell had attached itself to me, but I had to laugh at his reaction. And later, when I had time to sit and reflect over a beer after a shower, I laughed like Hell again, remembering the look on his face. But I had to ditch that suit! There was no way a dry cleaner could fix that, and frankly I didn't want the embarrassment of bringing it anywhere. As for the hearse, it took me weeks to get the car cleaned and free of that putrid smell.

Although decomp removals can be messy, we have had some bloody ones. They called us to a scene that was one of the messiest that I had ever seen. The medical examiner came in and cleared, so they released the individual directly to us. There was blood all over the floor, leaked out to the carpet into the hallway. Anyway, this guy was standing on his toilet, putting a hook into the ceiling, over the toilet. I'm not sure the intended purpose for the hook. Perhaps to hang a plant from the ceiling.

With the lid and the seat in the upright position, and this guy was standing on the bowl. The guy weighed over 200 pounds. The weight from his body and his stance cracked and broke the toilet. He came crashing down. The sharp porcelain cut him down to the artery and veins in his leg. He bled out before he could call or get help. The combination of the blood and water from the bowl combined, diluting the blood and the mixture of the two running everywhere. I'm sure it involved a lot of mopping in that bathroom, and a lot of carpet lost, because of the mess.

Another messy case of which I experienced was a gentleman who died in Florida back in the '90s. The person was living in an oceanfront condo. The area he was living in was under hurricane evacuation orders. He was on the 25th floor if I recall correctly. He stayed and did not evacuate with the others. He thought he had made the preparations necessary, but that was not the case. The hurricane came, blew out the sliding glass doors, and a large piece of glass flew into his thigh and severed his femoral artery. The poor guy had bled out and been dead for a day before they found him. Again, the combination of the water and the blood made for quite a mess.

Carbon monoxide deaths are a reality that most people only hear of and don't have to face. Some accidental, some suicide, but they always made me curious about what caused them or what caused someone to bring themselves to that point.

One summer morning, around 10 AM, they called us to a scene where it was an unattended death. The police were on site, and we were to pick up and transfer to the Medical Examiner's office. Upon arrival, we surveyed the route. It would require one of us to approach, talk to the officers, get the details, and walk the route, from the van to the decedent. You always want to make sure you have a clear path and move any obstructions or furniture that may be in the way.

Once inside, I made my way past the foyer upstairs, down the hall and into the bedroom. As I followed the officer, I looked around the bedroom. I noticed that there was a rolled-up towel on the floor near the door. One cop was finishing up photos, so I waited as to not get in his way. He said, "It's ok, come on in. I'm finished." There was a note on the floor, which was being tagged and bagged as I entered. The windows had duct tape on them. I wondered, "Why in the Hell were the windows taped shut?" Then I thought, well, I have seen crazier things. Maybe it was to keep the AC inside and the house cool. It was summer, and it was an older home.

The gentleman in question was lying on the bed, fully clothed, on top of the comforter. Not as if he had been sleeping. Not as if he had died during the night. Maybe he had laid down during the day for a nap, died the previous afternoon and was found this morning. Anything like that was possible. His color was not natural. He was very pink, which seemed unusual. Then, as I turned, I saw it. At the foot of the bed, on the floor, on top of a large cookie sheet, was a hibachi type grill. The type that you load with charcoal, light, and are suitable for maybe two steaks or four burgers. Not a large grill, but adequate. Then I realized. This bugger committed suicide. It all made sense.

He must have lit the grill outside and once the briquettes stopped smoking, he brought it inside the home, placing it on the cookie sheet as to not burn the home down. He wrote the note. Taped the windows closed. Stuffed the towel under the door, and laid down on the bed, for an eternal slumber, of which he would never wake. This was around the mid-Nineties, and I had seen a few suicides in my day, but I have to say, death by carbon monoxide was probably the cleanest form of suicide that I had seen to date, aside from overdose by prescription pills.

Another carbon monoxide death that stands out vividly in my memory is that of an elderly couple that used to live right across the street from the funeral home in Cotuit. This couple was the epitome of the sweetest couple ever.

They were both in their 70s. He had retired from a business career and her from a secretarial position. I believe that was how they met, and if I remember correctly, they had been married over forty years and had three children from that union. Just a loving, older couple that would always frequent the funeral home for a visitation or service, when it was one neighbor or someone from the small village. They knew just about everyone and were often seen out working in the yard or on their many walks around the neighborhood.

One Saturday night, we received a call, of which was another unattended death and a police call. I questioned the fact that they never gave me a name, but I jotted down the address and ran upstairs to put on a suit and tie. We always made removals in a suit and tie. If things were messy and we need to remove our jacket and roll up sleeves, then so be it.

As I drove to the funeral home, I kept repeating the location in my head. Damn, that address sounded familiar. And, as I was less than a mile away from the funeral home, it hit me. As I saw all the blue lights from the police cruisers, I knew exactly what the address was and who it was. My question was, which one? Was it he or she?

Thoughts rushed through my head. What could have happened? A slip and fall? A heart attack? Died in their sleep? And which one had died? Was it the husband or the wife? My god that would crush the other one. As I got the van loaded with a stretcher and prepared for my co-worker to arrive, the answering service called back. They had a call from the desk sergeant from the PD. I told them to patch it through to me, not a problem. He had stated that he forgot to say to me in the initial conversation that I needed two stretchers.

Now my mind is racing. What the Hell? Both Mr. and Mrs.? This loving couple that everyone in the community loved and adored? What could have happened? Was it a crime scene? What on Earth could it be?

As my co-worker arrived and parked, I informed him as we left the parking lot to drive across the street. He was in disbelief as was I. They had one of the loveliest landscaped homes in the area. They both took great pride in their yard and spent many hours in it, as one could tell by its appearance.

As we pulled into the driveway, one officer met us and said that he would move his car and we could back right up to the garage door, that they were both there. With that statement, my mind is going into overdrive.

Once backed up to the garage. We opened the rear of the van to get the stretchers ready. Again, we were to remove both individuals and drive them over to the Medical Examiner's Office on the Cape. They escorted me into the garage to examine the route, check the path, etc.

I saw nothing. I saw no body, let alone bodies on the floor. There was nothing, aside from a neatly organized garage, everything in its place, a single car in a two-car garage.

The supervising officer opened the door to the left rear seat. There, in the back of the car they were. He was dressed in a very nice suit and tie, and she was in a beautiful beige, full-length, sequin dress.

They looked as if they were the bride and groom on top of a cake. As if they had been to a formal event or such.

As I looked closer, I could see that both the complexions of each had a bright cherry-red color. There was an officer taking photos of everything and a note as he tagged and bagged it as evidence. Knowing the sergeant on the scene, we discussed what a lovely couple that they were. They were always so charming and so quick to chat with anyone, about anything. I remarked that I often heard them speak of their children, of which I believed lived in Boston.

He stated that it was because of the kids they did a welfare check. They called the kids that morning, and something just seemed out of sorts. The kids phoned one neighbor that evening and asked if someone could come over and check on them. When they didn't answer the door, the neighbor noticed the car in the garage through the window; they asked for a welfare check.

They left a note that they had written to the children. I asked him if I could read the note. He stated that he's not supposed to, and that I knew better than to ask. After asking a few more times, he finally agreed. He handed me the note, which was placed into a plastic evidence bag.

I wondered what the Hell he meant when he told me to go to my van and "Grab a few tissues before I read it." Afterward, I realized.

Dear Matthew, Sally, and Connie,

You know I am not one for long, drawn-out letters or speeches, so I will keep this brief.

There isn't a day that goes by that I am not constantly reminded that God has graced me and given me the eleven greatest treasures in this world.

When your mother and I laid eyes upon each other for the first time, it was magic. Yes, I know you have heard the story before, many times, but I love reliving it each time I tell it. We were complete in every way.

Then several years later, we were graced with each of you, the blessings that you three bestowed upon our lives, and each other's lives. As a family, we endured many years of love, some trials, some tribulations, but many years of loving, enjoyable memories.

Then as we grew older, you gave us the gift of seven loving grandchildren, whom we love dearly. As we got older, our pride in each of you became even more clear, as we saw what loving and nurturing parents you had become to your children.

You know your mother has been through the wringer for the last few years with her health and her cancer diagnosis. It has been a long hard road, of which you well know because you have been there throughout the journey. We all have. And it has taken its toll on her. She is the most courageous person I have ever had the privilege to know.

She has given it her all. Her weak, frail body can no longer take the effects that the radiation and chemo have placed upon her. And frankly, I am tired of seeing her suffer and hearing her cries of pain. It is hurting her and it is killing me.

Your mother's choice is that she wants to let go and slip away. My feelings are that I want to honor her wishes and I will not go on without my purpose in life and the woman I love!

We hope that you are all understanding and do not hate us for our decision. We love you all, more than anything in this world, but we feel that this for the best.

Everything you will need to take care of our affairs, etc., you will find in the filing cabinet in my study, at our safe deposit box at the bank and with our attorney, Jim Eddins.

Again, please don't have any hatred towards us for this decision.

Your loving parents,

Bob & Delores

Well, the Sergeant was right. I've only cried a handful of times in my life, but that was one of them. I returned it to him and walked over to the van where I could grab a tissue from the box we kept in our vehicle.

After a few minutes, we removed one stretcher from the car. We first placed her on the stretcher. In our usual manner, we would position the person on their back inside a light-duty, white body bag, or what we typically referred to as a pouch. We would then overlap the hands one over the other, close the pouch, and then secure the straps tightly as to hold the person in place on the cot. Once we had her into our vehicle, we did the same for the gentleman.

I remember making the comment that I wished we had a pouch and stretcher large enough for them both. After reading that note, I almost felt bad having to separate them.

As we left, I traveled down the street and turned to make my way to the Medical Examiner's Office. I thought to myself, "That was no letter; that was a testament of love. A proclamation of one man's passion and how powerful it was." The more I thought about it, the more I admired their relationship and who they were as a couple. Deep in my heart, I know there would be religious objections to what they did and how they handled things. Euthanasia is a tricky thing. We do it out of sympathy for our pets we love so dearly because we do not wish for them to suffer. For humans, society sees it differently. There will always be an argument for that topic. That is one that I haven't figured out yet.

While we are on a somber note, I have always found that dealing with the death of a child was always more difficult for me. I can handle death. I can handle the sight, feel, smell, morning, noon, night, seven days a week. But when there is the passing of a child, it hits hard.

It hits the parents, siblings, grandparents, family, friends, caregivers, and emergency personnel, and it hits the funeral home employees. Because we too have children, grandchildren, nieces, and nephews. I've always tried to do my best to surpass any experience that I could give a parent. Whether it is in trying to ensure that I do my best embalming job on a child. To take away the pain of the circumstance to make it so they can hold their son or daughter one last time. To have the perfect lullabies or music playing when they see them for the first time after a misfortune.

One cold winter morning when I worked in Worcester, we were called to a home by a hospice nurse to pick up a five-year-old boy who had died of leukemia. The embalmer I studied under, Bill and I chatted on the way over. Par for the course, we may have shared a laugh or two on the drive. Bill was always full of jokes and tales. As we turned onto the street, we confirmed the number of the house, from the paper I had in hand. We had a little difficulty backing into the driveway. It had snowed the previous night, and the driveway was not shoveled. It was only about 4 inches of snow, but it made it difficult to differentiate between driveway and the lawn.

As I sat and pondered, I thought about how shoveling the driveway would usually be the first thing on my mind, but if it were my child that had died, I would probably be inseparable from their side at that given moment. I would want to sit there and hold them. I would want to sit and old their hand and not let go, even though I knew deep down that I should.

I waited in the car as Bill ventured into the home to talk to the family. As he returned, I exited the vehicle. We grabbed the stretcher and make our way into the house, as the hospice nurse led the way. I was careful to kick and shake any snow from my shoes as we entered. As we entered the bedroom, I noticed quite a collection of stuffed animals. They also decorated the bedroom with a rainbow pattern wallpaper. He was a wee little man, dressed in his pajamas and holding a stuffed animal. Both parents stayed in the bedroom as we conveyed him from the comfort of his bed to the cot. Mom asked if we could keep that stuffed animal with him, as it was his favorite. We said we would make sure it remained with him. She assured us she would bring in a new one for the viewing. One more presentable than that one, which showed signs of wear. Bill assured her she should use whichever one she thought would please him more.

From the instance we placed that little man onto the stretcher, it's almost like things abruptly changed. From that moment forward, I said nothing, and Bill only spoke nine words. "The family said they want an open casket viewing."

We drove back the funeral home. Upon arrival, we removed the stretcher from the hearse, wheeled into the prep room, and placed him onto the embalming table. I removed his pajamas, careful to not cut anything, in case they wanted them back. Bill looked him over for a few seconds, walked over to the cabinet and selected his choice of fluids, and we went to work. We were taking longer than any other embalming that we have done for an adult. We were meticulous. I must have checked and compared every fingernail on that child to make sure they were the same length, that his appearance was right and that he had optimum clearing and color, during the embalming process.

For what seemed like hours, which it wasn't, Bill and I finished, bathed, and dried this young fellow. We would typically just cover the deceased in a sheet, but not this time. As I grabbed the clean pajamas that he arrived in, I began dressing him back into them. It was as if Bill had read my mind, and that was the most respectful thing to do. Once dressed, we were not done until we tucked the stuffed animal under his arm and joined his hands together, almost as if he was cradling it. When his parents brought in the clothing, we dressed him and placed him in the casket, cradling his favorite stuffed animal in his arms.

You might be a big, strong man who is a badass. But, when a mom sees her child for the first time after death and is pleased with his appearance so much that she comes over to hug you and almost chokes you crying tears of sorrow, pain but joy at how he resembles himself. It'll kick you in the stomach and make you a blubbering, weeping mess.

Many people get into the funeral profession for different reasons, but the joy you get from helping someone at one of the most challenging times in their life is what it is all about. Taking the time to embalm and prepare someone so that the family can have that closure and time to say goodbye is truly a good feeling.

Another instance of child death and a complicated circumstance was a family that had lost their child because of a lawnmower accident. Their son was about three years old. His parents described him as a "happy child." He loved to play, laugh, and to be around his parents. His dad would go out and mow the yard, and the little one would push around his bubble mower as he would emulate Dad. Even though Dad had a riding mower, he would push his mower outside, just like the dad.

I don't know the complete circumstances, but I guess dad pulled up to a tree, the tike had run up behind him, dad didn't see him and backed up.

I am glad I did not have to make the arrangements on that death. I can imagine what a delicate condition both parents would be. However, I had the task of embalming. It was horrific even to think about the state of the young lad. Surprising enough, trauma and bruising were at a minimal degree and less severe than I thought. I embalmed him, spending extra time and care to the back of his skull, where the damage was primarily,

Many times with any reconstruction or restorative art, as some refer to it, there are several steps. First, you would embalm for the preservation aspect. Then you would come back and complete your sealing and restoration of the area after things have dried.

When all was said and done, I would have to say that we did a good job. We even asked the parents to bring in a small ball cap, which worked out well on concealing some apparent damage. The parents were happy that they could see him, and the rest of the family. I still wonder if the parents are still together to this day. That can be one Hell of a thing to live with for the rest of your life. I'm not saying that the mother blamed the father because I do not know that to be the case. But I can see where any mother might. I can see where any father might blame himself and where that could crumble a marriage.

On a lighter note, one day, I was called to the Medical Examiner's Office, back on the Cape. We had just purchased a new minivan that we used for removals. It only had a couple of hundred miles on it and was a dark midnight blue, which matched the rest of our fleet. As I arrived, it was business as usual. Walk-in, greet everyone, give the name of the deceased you are there to pick up. Once brought out to you on a gurney from the cooler, you transfer to your stretcher from the gurney. They return the gurney to the cooler. You confirm identity via the ankle bracelet. You're given personal effects, and you sign for personal effects. Not that hard. The personals are in a bag just like one receives when being discharged from the hospital, which is a white and blue plastic bag, labeled Patient's Belongings. I took said bag, which only had clothing in it, as far as I assumed and placed it into the back of the van, beside the stretcher and began my thirty-minute drive back to the funeral home.

As I make my way down the road, I heard some strange noise. I turned down the radio, and it appeared to be more of a rattle. I pulled over. I checked for oncoming cars and opened the driver's door, trying to see if it was coming from under the vehicle which it appeared to be. Once I exited and got under the van, I could not hear it. I jumped back into the vehicle. I heard nothing, so I closed the door and pulled back onto the roadway.

A few miles down the road, again I began to hear the noise. Again, I pulled over, turned down the radio. I tried to pinpoint from where in the Hell this rattle was coming. This time it sounded like a metallic rattle. It almost seemed like when the weld breaks on a heat shield on your exhaust system or a catalytic convertor. I spent another five to ten minutes trying to hear or find it — still nothing. Again, I pulled back onto the roadway, trying to make my way back to the funeral home.

One more time, this irritating rattle started. I pulled over and turned the radio off. I listened. I got under the van, and I listened. This time I walked around to the back of the van and lifted the rear cargo door. I continued to listen. As I looked under the stretcher, I saw what appeared to be the Patient's Belongings bag. It had slid under the stretcher. I reached under and pulled the bag out. It was the bag that was rattling. I did not understand what the Hell was going on, what was making the damn bag rattle, and frankly, I was a little freaked out to want to look inside.

As I slowly, carefully grabbed and opened the bag, wondering if it was a damn rattlesnake or something crazy like that, I saw the culprit. There, inside the bag, along with a floral silk robe, was a pink vibrator, buzzing, humming, rattling and making every other sound that I heard as I was driving. I was like, What in the Hell is going on? All I want to do is finish my day and go home.

Back at the funeral home, I unloaded the stretcher and personal effects. I logged the young lady into our morgue log, completed a few other pieces of paperwork, and I placed the bag onto the countertop in our prep room and picked up the nearby phone. As I dialed the number at the ME's office, it surprised me I got anyone as it was almost closing time there.

When I heard mike's voice on the other end of the line, I said, "Ha Ha Asshole, you got me. Very funny! But I'm going to tell you this, paybacks are a Bitch!"

His response was puzzled, as he claimed he did not understand what I was speaking about. "The vibrator, the one you put in the bag of belongings, trying to mess with me!", I said.

After a five-second pause, he responded, "Kevin, that's hers. It came in with her. She was having an intimate moment at home, and apparently, she suffered a very intense cardiac episode."

I was astounded. In as many years, I had never heard that one. I apologized to Mike and hung the phone up, still trying to fathom the possibilities of said demise.

After a few minutes of thought, I took the patient's belongings bag, removed the robe, and placed it into one of our personal's bags to give to the family. I put the one with the vibrator on top of one cabinet in the prep room. I figured I would wait six to nine months and if it never came up, I would toss it. There is no way I would hand that to the parents unless they came asking for it. They never did.

Often when making removals, we work with other agencies on the scene, such as hospice, nursing home employees, law enforcement. One instance of picking up at home at an unattended death brings to mind the story of an unhappy deputy.

We had been called out to a mobile home in Fort Walton Beach a few years ago. Once we were on site, I spoke with the deputy who stated that they had located the name and telephone number of the next of kin and placed a call to them. The sheriff's department instructed that their office had released to us and that they should contact us at the funeral home. Because of the person's health history, the medical examiner had waived jurisdiction, and we were to reach out to the primary care physician to sign the death certificate.

The deputy led me inside the dwelling so I could check the route and as usual, make sure there were no obstacles we needed to move. As I looked around, I noticed that there was a trail of body fluids. The trail led from a living room chair to the bedroom. Then, from the bedroom into the bathroom. Then from the bathroom into the kitchen and then back to the bathroom. The appearance of the fluids looked to be purge from the stomach and diarrhea. Stomach purge is a collective term amongst embalmers which refers to a liquid that has a coffee-ground appearance, sour odor, contains acid and usually exits through the nose and mouth. It can be quite messy and create nasty stains that sometimes may or may not be cleaned.

From appearances, it looked as if she was sitting in her recliner began to feel ill, ran to the bathroom, became scared and confused, running back to the kitchen and then back to the bathroom again, where she collapsed and died in a fetal position onto the bathroom floor.

As I exited and got my co-worker and the stretcher, we entered the home, went to the bathroom floor. We collapsed the stretcher to the floor beside her. After we opened a pouch onto the stretcher, we placed her inside and flexed her arms and legs to ease the rigor mortis. Afterward, putting her into a more respectable position with her hands overlapped onto her abdomen. It not only made the person more comfortable to carry on the stretcher. It also made things more manageable in case we were to embalm at a later time.

Once we had her on the stretcher, I told my partner to standby as I went into the kitchen to see if I could find any paper towels, of which I could not. As I checked under the sink for cleaning supplies, I could see that the deputy was checking his watch. Once I had a few bottles of cleaning supplies in hand, I turned to address the body fluids on the kitchen floor. I heard the deputy ask, "What are you doing?" as he continued to check his watch. I turned and stated that I would spray some cleaner on the kitchen floor and the bathroom floor to clean up some of the mess. He responded that he needed to secure the scene and leave. By my estimate was that it was nearing four o'clock, which was the end of his shift and he needed us out of there.

So, I responded that I would spray the floors, let it sit and soak, as we carried this woman out to the car. Once out, I would have my partner wait in the car with the decedent, as I came back in to clean the floor. Again, he started in with "I need to leave. You both need to leave so I can secure the scene."

Seeing where this was going, and fearful that he would probably lock the door once we were outside, I pumped a few more sprays of the cleaning material onto both floors and told my partner to standby. I responded to the deputy. "I'm cleaning this floor. You can leave, you can stay, you do what you need to do. I don't care either way. It will not kill you to wait five minutes for me to clean what I can. I can't do anything about the carpet, but I can clean this linoleum. And if this were your family member, you would probably be appreciative if someone at least attempted to help you."

As his jaw dropped a little, I kept right on with my whirlwind of trying to hurry. I spotted some old towels under the sink which I ran back to retrieve and use as cleaning cloths. I turned on the washing machine and threw in some soap. As I had exhausted the few towels and gotten the last bit up, I made my way over to the washer. I chucked them in. I closed the lid and prayed that they came clean.

As we wheeled past the deputy who was ready to close and lock the door, I said, "Thank You," as he nodded to me.

When the family came into the funeral home, I was the director that met with them. Upon walking them out, they stated that they were headed over to Mom's house. I told them to be sure to check the washer that there would be towels in there from the previous day that needed to go into the dryer but to check them first for cleanliness. The daughter turned and said, "Thank You, that was very kind."

Sometimes the least little action can make a big difference in someone's day or even life. It feels good to make a difference.

As stated before, you never know what you're walking into when you show up to make a removal. Many factors can determine that. And in this case, it would be one of God's furry little creatures.

One Saturday night, years ago back on Cape Cod, dispatch called us to an unattended death at a residence. Again, not too far from the funeral home. We arrived at the address which was on the mailbox. I knew this was the spot from the police cruiser in the driveway. Well, what appeared as a driveway. It was a dirt driveway that was highly eroded over time and uneven. They instructed us to pull around the corner to a small clearing at the base of the driveway. The clearing was not visible to the traffic on the main road. There was a pick-up truck marked with blue lights on top and police department logos on the sides. The officer told us that there was little chance that we could climb the driveway in our vehicle and that we should probably place our stretcher into the back of the pick-up and ride up in the truck.

As we rode up the steep and washed out driveway, I had asked if they had a cargo strap or two onboard. It was bumpy, and I could see the nightmare of the stretcher turning over in the truck's bed. The driver stated that he had several and it should not be a problem.

Once at the top of the driveway, we circled back around to the back porch of the house. As we drove past the front porch, I noticed that there was so much stuff piled up that you couldn't even see the door. Hence why they brought us to the rear of the house. The back was not much better. We exited the truck and made our way into the house. To say the house was full of clutter would be an understatement.

As I saw only flashlights illuminating the inside of the home by the officers on the scene, I remarked to myself, "This will be fun." I asked what was going on with no power; they said the gentleman was a recluse. He had one or two distant family members that lived out of state. There was no water or electricity in the home, and it would be fair to say that he was a hoarder.

It was about that time that the smell hit me like a Louisville Slugger to the face. I had remarked, "What in the Hell is that smell?" Although I am sure I knew what it was, my question was, why did I smell it? The stench was a combination of urine and fecal material that was both old and in significant amounts. I would ask why no one opened a window, but from limited visibility of just the flashlights, I could tell that a few of the windows in the home were missing. The officer stated that it would appear that with no water, this gentleman was using five-gallon buckets as his toilet and would walk them outside and empty them. As his health got worse, one could only guess that he could no longer make it out to empty them, and just let them accumulate.

As they led us over to where the man had collapsed onto the floor, we lowered the stretcher to the floor, just beside him. I didn't notice at first, but once the flashlight had shown on him, I could tell his left radius and ulna, and right tibia and fibula had no meat on them. I mean they were cleaned right down to the bone! Cleaner and brighter than any skeleton that anyone has ever seen hanging in an anatomy classroom.

I asked the cop, "What the Hell Happened? Where did the rest of him go?" The officer said, "We're not positive, but we think these fellows had a little to do with that. It looks as they even picked on his face a little." The officer then moved his flashlight to a raccoon that was making his way out of one window. He stated that the place was crawling with raccoons when they made their way into the home. "If we were a few weeks later in finding him, there would probably be only bones left.

As we got him into a pouch and onto the stretcher, I could only think about one thing. I want to get the Hell out of here, get home, get naked, into the shower, and scrub this funky smell off myself. My skin was crawling!

Once down to the bottom of the driveway, we transferred him to our car. Made our way back to the funeral home and tucked him away. I drove home with the windows down, trying to air my clothes out.

I had a routine when I arrived home after any time that I had a stinker removal. I kept a stash of clean, folded old towels in my workshop in the garage. I would disrobe and place my suit and tie onto a hanger to air out in the backyard before taking it to the dry cleaners, purely out of embarrassment of the smell. I would start the washing machine and load everything else into it that could be laundered. I would then wrap the towel around me and make my way directly to the shower where I would use a liberal amount of soap and a scrub brush to fight the funk. Sometimes I wanted to use an SOS pad, but I knew better! But that's how bad it smelled sometimes. Sometimes, even after a long shower, scrubbing my nostrils and brushing my teeth, the taste of a beer would seem compromised.

There is an adage that people in the South often use. Especially when they have to deal with such smells on the job. Whether their occupation is working at a paper mill, a sewage-related field, a chicken house, stockyard or in the healthcare field where there might be some unpleasantries, you can always hear one person use the term "Smells like money to me!" And that is what you have to say to yourself occasionally to get through it.

It smells like money to me. Someone is paying me to put up with this. Let's make some money; we can shower and clean up afterward.

Another vital part of the funeral process is the arrangement conference. Often this is the first face-to-face contact with the funeral director or funeral home. It is intended to meet with the next of kin or the family to make the arrangements for whatever the family or decedent might have chosen as the final disposition. It can a challenge in the aspect that you are dealing with a family at a challenging and emotional time. You need to be receptive and understanding of their questions, ideas, and concerns.

I have always commented that Funerals will either mend relationships in a family or ultimately burn bridges to the ground, and I have seen it for over thirty years. Often the funeral arranger is hit with some rather unusual requests. You find out which set of family members do not get along with other family members, and sometimes you can see some downright nasty fights. It has never ceased to amaze me at the lengths that people will go to in order to make others feel angry or hurt them. Quotes like "I'm not attending if this person will be there." "You never cared or loved them." "They didn't care or love you." "I am not allowing them to attend the services." "I'm not mentioning that person or her children in the obituary." "That side of the family may not view the body."

Crazy, incredible statements that you would imagine no one saying. I'm also talking about fighting over assets, who is getting what, who may distribute the assets. I have even seen where someone has had to sit at home and guard the decedent's belongings during the arrangements, visitation, services, and burial, for fear that someone would help themselves while the others were not there. On more than several instances, I have stood up at an arrangement conference and had to say, "I will excuse myself and step outside while you continue this. When you finish and are ready to get serious, we can finish planning this funeral. I'm sure (your mother or father) would not be happy about this behavior."

Many times things have a way of working themselves out, and many times it escalates. I've even had to get between family members to break up fights in the funeral home and inadvertently gotten hit with a few punches over the years.

Several years ago in Fort Walton Beach, I had a family come into view a young lady before her cremation. It was a group of about ten people, mostly siblings of the young lady and her mother. As was the case where there was a rift in the family, which was clear, I truly felt sorry for the mother who was appropriately grieving the loss of her daughter. It's never the natural order of things that children should pass before a parent does.

I could tell that the mother was having a tough time. I walked her into the room, and I pulled up a chair so she could sit close to and hold her daughter's hand. You could get that vibe that the manner, tone, and volume of those in the room that they were just not sympathetic to the mother and her feelings. Almost as if they were there to spite others but no sympathy for how she was taking the loss of her daughter.

Both I and the funeral home associate that was working with me ventured down the hall to give them a little privacy. About 10 minutes later as we were talking, I heard a rather loud sound, distinctive of the sound that you hear when someone is being shoved into a wall. Upon hearing that, we looked at each other and hurried to the doorway of the room where we observed a scuffle that had broken out — one person yelling at another. A third person was yelling at them — one gentleman, who had another in a headlock. As I quickly went in, I raised my voice telling them to stop. I grabbed the arm of the one starting the headlock and released the other man's head. I was positioning myself between them. The recipient of the headlock then threw a punch at the other. After a few seconds, the mother began crying louder and harder after that.

I raised my voice yelling, "Hey, knock that it off and have some respect for your mother!" As for some of them, it could have been some of their mother-in-law for all I know, but it got my point across. "I'll call the sheriff's department and have them haul all of your asses out of here except for your mother, and she'll be the only one allowed to view and spend time with your sister."

As I walked over to the mom, I picked up a box of tissues and extended it outward to her. She took two and as I placed the box onto a table as I walked out. You could hear a pin drop.

It was a hushed hour after that. The family had finally had enough time with the young lady and had started to make their way out, down the hall to the foyer. Almost every person in that group stopped and said: "We're sorry about that." My response was, "It happens. No one's perfect. You probably need to be more receptive to how your mom is feeling." The mother stopped and gave me the biggest hug and said: "Thank You."

Years ago I had an appointment to meet with a woman who had lost her husband. He was around the age of the late '40s and was a business executive. We had transported him back to Cape Cod from out of state where he died. As I greeted her at the door, I introduced myself and took the garment bags that she was carrying. As I led her down the hallway to the office, I had hung up the larger garment bag on the coat rack in the hallway. We then proceeded into the office where we would make the arrangements.

The other bag was a paper grocery type bag with the handles on top, which I placed on one chair. As I looked in the bag, I was a little puzzled. What caught my eye was silky and shiny. As I looked back in thinking it was boxers, it was not. As I looked back in and staring to confirm what I thought was a garter belt, bra, and panties. I was correct. Thinking they handed me the wrong bag, I turned to the wife, and before I could ask, she interjects with "I know, I know, I'm not happy about it. But that is him, that is what he wanted, and I'm honoring his wishes."

I walked around and sat in my chair behind the desk. picked up my pen, and looked her in the eyes saying, "And what type of arrangements were you thinking of?" I think she was a little taken back at my relaxed manner in which I addressed the women's clothing, but it was none of my business.

Embalming is the art and science of preserving human remains by treating them (in its modern form with chemicals) to delay decomposition. The intention is usually to make the deceased suitable for viewing as part of the funeral ceremony or keep them preserved for medical purposes. The three goals of embalming are sanitization, presentation, and preservation. Embalming dates to the Egyptians back before 2600 BC and became popular here in the states during the 1860s.

Every embalmer has stories that they can share with you about embalming. Some stories are sad, some funny, some not for the squeamish and some only for those of us in the business.

For 18 months, I worked as an embalmer at a Care Center, as we commonly refer it to at some corporate funeral homes. The Care Center is the facility that performs the embalming, dressing, and cosmetics for several area corporate funeral homes. Once a person is embalmed, prepared, and placed into a casket, we send them to the funeral home of choice for their viewing or service, or sometimes to a church instead.

The care center I worked at handled roughly 800 embalmings a year. For a brief time, I had an assistant who helped with some cosmetics, but I mostly handled the embalmings. There was a young fellow that worked at the funeral home where the care center was that used to say "Kevin's record for embalmings is nine in one day, and four of them before lunch." But I have to admit, there were two tables, and sometimes I would tag Team. Two tables, two machines, and I could inject two simultaneously, keeping a careful eye on both and monitoring results.

But anyone that knows me will tell you I take no shortcuts with the embalming job or a client's appearance. There are many things we do in the Back Room to serve a purpose, that most people need not know, nor would they understand. I always try to speak with the utmost delicacy and respect in my descriptions of such things.

Everyone's body tells a story! Scars from injury. Tattoos from one's life experiences or adventures in a faraway land. Loss of a digit or limb from working in a hazardous occupation to place food on the table. The sometimes damaged body of a veteran that occurred in the line of duty during wartime. The crooked fingers of an older woman that worked in a factory for years.

When embalming, I often would look and wonder at the human body, and the stories told. I would try to gain insight into someone's life and who they were. Just as I would from reading an obituary and hearing the stories shared of their life.

There are many obstacles we find when preparing the body for burial. There are many tricks of the trade. The chemicals we use each have their intended purpose. Some are a humectant, some a desiccant, some to add color and some as a corrective water measure. There are liquid chemicals and powdered chemicals. I've used plaster to repair the cranial area. I've used PVC pipe to reconstruct limbs, and to assist with a person's appearance, wire coat hanger and newspaper in the trousers to make a sharp crease in men's pants, cotton padding over the shoulders and abdomen to replace lost weight, and into bras to add that bit of "Perky" back to the bosoms. We do what we do, based on what we need. There are even products marketed by the embalming companies called tissue builder, which is the equivalent of Botox for the deceased. It is very helpful for adding a fuller appearance back to someone that has suffered drastic weight loss because of an illness.

One morning I arrived for work, and I checked the roster to see how many embalmings I had before me. One of said was a young man in his 20s who was involved in a motor vehicle accident on Christmas Eve, attempting to join his parents at Midnight Mass. We had received his body from the Medical Examiner's office, and they informed me that the family had wanted an open casket. My first response was my usual response, which was, "They know that he was in a car accident, right?" So, I unzipped the bag, positioned the patient onto the embalming table, and began my work. It was challenging because of his injuries and the fact that
he had been decapitated. It would appear that he had lost control of his car and driven under a tractor-trailer.

I embalmed the decedent as I usually would embalm anyone who has had an autopsy. The only difference is that I had to preserve the head separately from the body. With the patient's head being separated, I had to allow both the neck above the chest and the neck below the head to dry with the use of chemicals. It was only after drying out thoroughly that I could use a sealant. As I dried and sealed both areas, it was time to marry the two.

As luck would have it, the area of the severance was almost a clean, even cut and located just below where the collar of the shirt would ride. Great! I could conceal the damage with the shirt collar. That worked to my advantage. I dried all the abrasions and lacerations to the face and sealed them in the same manner.

I worked tirelessly for hours on this guy. I was waxing each sealed abrasion and laceration. I airbrushed the skin to the right shade with a foundation, then with cosmetics. I powdered after with a tinted cosmetic powder to lose the sheen and applied just the correct amount of lip color, bumping it down where the lip line meets the face, Long hours, straight through and wheeled him into place, one and a half-hour before the family arrived.

Once I dimmed, then raised, then dimmed the lights to where they needed to be. Trust me; every embalmer will sit there fussing with the lights and cosmetics like an obsessive-compulsive for at least six times before a family comes in on a severe case. I was ready. Some employees came in and observed the young man lying in state. I cringed at the verdict from each. They were optimistic about their opinions. I was nervous. When the family arrived, they walked into the chapel where the casket was closed and decided that they would keep it that way.

In the beginning, they did not want to open the casket for the public but were adamant that they wished to view their son. They had changed their minds. And it was probably for the best. Many times I have advised against a family viewing their loved one after a devastating accident. Sometimes that advice is heeded. Sometimes it is not. This time it was. I was a little put out at first that they chose not to view after I had spent countless hours to make it possible. But, deep down I knew it was in their best interest not to, and in my heart, I knew I gave it my best. And that is what matters.

In one instance, I had a gentleman that died as the result of a drug overdose and was not found for several weeks. I met with the father who was adamant that he would view his son prior to the cremation.

I explained the circumstances to the gentleman about the condition of his son repeatedly, but he was going to view his son and would not be convinced otherwise. I agreed to his request, again stressing to him I recommended against it and had him sign a waiver that we were not liable for any effects, both psychological or physical, of said viewing.

The father questioned why we would do the viewing at the crematory and not in the funeral home. Again, I explained to they had not found him for weeks. That there was decomposition and the smell, and we were not exposing the interior of the funeral home to that. We would do it at the crematory.

I made every attempt to make it as pleasing of an experience that I could. I posed the son's facial features in a manner as to his being asleep or at rest. I used every conceivable deodorizing spray that I could think of to mask the smell and explained to him he would be only viewing from the chin to the eyebrows, because of the autopsy procedure. That made it a little easier in that I covered all but his face with a sheet. The sheet made things better, in that I could saturate the cloth with a deodorizing liquid.

I gave the father the time he needed. I was within eyesight, assuring him I was there if needed but far enough away to give him privacy. Afterward, he thanked me for the opportunity and my efforts. He stated that he wished that he had listened to my recommendation of not viewing. I told him I wished he had. But sometimes we need to see things for ourselves. If he needed that for closure, I was understanding, but many times that final vision is the one we live with forever.

Often when we have someone in our care, preparing them for their services, we notice things that others don't. Several times over the years, I have called the medical examiner's office to apprise them of a bruise, discoloration, fracture, etc. You want them to know of anything that they should be to do their job. This time I was calling them to come to pick up a handgun.

The death call came in the previous night. A woman who had died at home in Pensacola, in her sleep. She was elderly and had a medical history, and the medical examiner was notified but had waived jurisdiction to the funeral home. Our removal people had picked up, transferred to the funeral home and placed her in our cooler. I was not the one who met with the family but they informed me she needed to be embalmed.

I transferred the woman to a stretcher from a shelf in our cooler, and I wheeled her over to the embalming table. As I placed my hands under her back to pull her over from the stretcher to the table, I felt something hard, under the small of her back. As I felt again, I knew what that object was. I carefully removed one hand, lifting her slightly so I could remove my other hand without pulling it from under her. As I rolled her over, I could see that she was lying on top of a revolver. Since my hand was gloved, I picked it up by the grip and placed it into a large plastic bag that we used for cremated remains.

I then had to put my embalming on hold and call the medical examiner's office. I had informed them that the call that they waived had a 38 revolver under her, which was transferred with her into our care. They stated that they would send over a tech to examine her visually, retrieve the gun, and it would take about an hour to get someone over to us.

Once there, they rolled and examined her; They ruled out the fact of whether she had been shot. The investigators on the scene concluded that it was a natural death. The decedent merely slept with the gun under her pillow. They had scooped it up in the sheet when the removal crew had brought her to the funeral home. I mentioned to her that "Yeah, it's usual that you slide your gloved hand under someone to lift and pull backward onto the stretcher. It's a good thing they didn't pull a trigger when pulling backward, and that someone could have gotten shot." She agreed.

Often the embalmer faces challenges with nature or condition on the subject's body that we are tasked to embalm. I've always commented that hospitals, etc. are doing too much to keep people alive that it sometimes does more harm to the body than good. Hospitals are famous for pumping the body full of fluids and medications. It significantly takes its toll on the person's appearance. Many times when the funeral home receives the body, there is massive swelling and severe fluid retention. Sometimes it may be corrected or minimized; many times, it can't. Yes, it keeps the person alive longer, and often it is so that the hospital can keep charging the insurance company or payor. If you don't believe that, look at how often the hospital is so quick to ship someone off to a rehab or nursing home after the money has run out.

As an embalmer, often we are required to look at these conditions and sometimes feel like a mixologist. Carefully adding a specific embalming fluid for color, another one for firming and a third for displacing moisture. Each usually has its specific purpose and you must know which will work together and which will not. After a few years, you kind of have it down to a science and could do it blindfolded or in your sleep.

Often we deal with physical obstacles other than the condition of the patient or attributed to an act of God as one might say.

Several years ago, in the early evening, I had an embalming to accomplish before I left for the day. There was a torrential rainstorm lingering like it did not intend to leave soon. So, I thought I would do the embalming, stay dry, and in about an hour, after I had finished, it should be over.

I had just gotten the person on the embalming table in the right position. I posed the features and had gotten them to my satisfaction. I had washed them; he was shaved, and I had made my incision for insertion and drainage on the skin over the clavicle. Suddenly there was a loud crackle of thunder outside, and then the lights went out. Damnit man. We had lost power. Now I was really in a jam, as I already had a full day of a funeral, arrangements and a visitation the following day. There was no way I could factor in an embalming too.

I waited, and I expected, but still, no power came back on. After a while, an idea entered my mind. It was something that my embalming professor had mentioned one day in class, and it always hung in the back of my mind. He once stated that the old "Portiboy" style embalming machines could be operated without power. That they worked in a similar manner as the gravity flow system. And, with the electricity not coming back on, I might as well try it. Sitting and waiting were not getting this embalming completed.

I grabbed a flashlight and made my way to the garage. After about ten minutes of rummaging around, I located a 10-foot ladder, a small piece of plywood, a drill, and several drywall screws. I made my way back to the prep room, careful not to trip and kill myself in the dark, with all that crap in my hands. As I made sure the ceiling was high enough, which it was, I put the ladder in place. I then screwed the plywood to the top and made my way down the ladder. I found a five-gallon bucket that I emptied the embalming fluid from, Into the machine.

I carried the machine to the top of the ladder and onto the makeshift tabletop. I then came back down to grab the bucket. Carefully as to not drench myself in the nearly two-and-a-half gallons of carcinogenic liquid I was carrying, I made it back up and emptied the bucket into and placed the lid on the machine.

I just had about three inches to spare on the length of hose running from the machine that is used to embalm the patient. As I twisted the petcock to the end of the hose, I held my breath for a moment to see whether it would work or if I had wasted my time and would scream so loudly that the whole neighborhood would hear me.

It worked. I quickly and carefully, as I had limited vision in this lighting, raised the carotid artery, snipped, slid in the cannula, and clamped it off. I then cut the jugular vein with my scissors and twisted the petcock to the on position. As the gravity was doing its job, I placed a suction cup hose holder onto the table, turned the faucet on slightly and let the trickle of water do its thing.

I seem to remember our professor stating that for every foot above the deceased individual, the gravity feed would administer approximately one-half pound of pressure. So, with the table being in the lowest position, that put the top of the ladder at about seven feet above the top of the table, equating to about 3.5 pounds of pressure. That's about 2.5 pounds less than my preference. So, I once again climbed the ladder and added just a few more ounces of fluid, only to be on the safe side. Osmosis was good, but at that pressure, I wanted just a little more strength to the liquid.

First, I saw the arteries and veins in the hands stand up. Then I saw the same in the arms and lower legs. Not like you would typically see with the machine in full-electric mode, but a slight change. This would take time. I ventured back into the funeral home, to the front of the building where I could see a flashing yellow light on the road. Yep, it was the Power Company bucket truck, and they were replacing a transformer that had taken a hit from the storm.

I grabbed a beverage, sat down and took a break. After about 45 minutes, I returned to the prep room and found that the injection of the lower extremities looked good, but still had a while to go. I returned about 30 minutes later. I removed the cannula, tied off the lower part of the artery, and placed the cannula into the upper portion of the artery. As I twisted the petcock to allow the flow, I began to soap up and wash the gentleman. After about fifteen minutes, that portion was complete. I drained the last bit of fluid left in the machine, washed, rinsed, re-filled the water in the machine and recoiled the hose around the glass tank. I would wait until the next morning and complete the last of the embalming, comprising the aspiration. The time-sensitive portion was complete. Many embalmers wait until the next day to complete the aspiration. I could never understand that ideology, but some old-timers I have known over the years swear by that practice to this day. I would not go probing around in a dimly lit area, with a long sword-like instrument, taking the risk of running through my hand with it. They should have the power restored in the morning, and it can wait until then.

Speaking of storms, they can be quite a pain in the ass for other instances. Hurricanes can be troublesome as you often have to maintain the refrigeration of the deceased individuals in your care. If you lose power for an extended amount of time, you better have a contingency plan, such as a generator in place. I think every funeral director or embalmer has had the nightmare where they think about "what if the power goes out or the refrigeration fails?" Many people might say, "Oh Well! You're dead. What's it going to hurt?" The problem is, deep down in your heart, you would not want that to happen to anyone's loved one. Let alone anyone's loved one that was entrusted into your care. But, should that rapid form of decomp happen, especially to someone that was to be embalmed and displayed for a viewing or open casket service, that could be a huge mistake that any attorney would leap at these days. Truthfully people will sue over just about anything. And, as a funeral director, there is even more room for opportunity than in some other professions.

On one occasion, we lost power at a visitation preceding a service. The funeral home wasn't packed with occupants, but there was a fair amount of people. I announced that we had lost power. I began by "Ladies and gentlemen if I could have your attention. Because of the weather, we have lost electricity, as have some of our neighbors. I assure you we have paid our power bill. (Everyone laughed) If you give us just a few minutes, we will come around and be placing candles in the room. I only ask that everyone keep an eye out so that the little ones don't play with the candles. Thank You."

I asked one of our directors who I knew played the guitar if he had it with him. He stated that he had an acoustic guitar in his car, wasn't involved with anything at that moment, and he would bring it in and play. Once he returned, the room was still filled with people who were talking amongst themselves. He broke into a round of acoustic hymns that later evolved into a few requests from the family that were favorites of the deceased.

Sometimes things have a way of working out the way they do for a reason. As people were leaving, I tried to make it a point to apologize for the trouble with the power. Just about everyone that was leaving, including the family, stopped on their way out, stated what a lovely service it was, and how fitting it was for the moment. What we see as a nightmare sometimes makes for a more memorable moment for the family. So much in fact, that we buried that woman's husband about five years later. And, during the arrangement conference, the family brought up the series of events, stated that they wanted us to dim the lights, and have the service by candlelight, just like we had done for Mom.

Back on Cape Cod, not only did we have the hurricanes to worry about, but we also had blizzards and Nor' easters of which to contend. Frequently, we had to work around having a funeral or a visitation during a snowstorm, and you can't postpone or reschedule something like that. Especially if you have people from out of town or no availabilities with the funeral home, sometimes we were booked up for a whole week at a time and couldn't move the service to another day. I've seen the family come into a night visitation, see the snow accumulate and decide that they will head home and forgo the last hour of visitation, to make it home safe.

Occasionally, we would get a call for a removal. The roads had not been plowed yet, or capable of travel because of snow. Many times we would tell the hospice nurse that they would have to raise the window a few inches, close the bedroom door and place a rolled-up towel under the door to cool the room that the patient was in, yet keep the heat in the rest of the house. "We'll get there just as quickly as permitted by the police and the road crews." The funeral home also had the removal wagon/van and hearse in a garage below, which was considered basement level. It had a steep ramp to get up on the morning of a funeral or in the middle of the night, should we have a removal. None of us looked forwarding to shoveling, but we knew it was a necessary evil to shovel, salt and sand so we could get either vehicle up the hill.

Snowstorms were always an inconvenience for work, but they made a great day of play for the kids. Back in the '90s, I had my private station wagon and later my minivan registered as a hearse. According to Massachusetts law, to convey a deceased human body, it required registering the vehicles as a hearse with the Department of Motor Vehicles and your insurance carrier. I had picked up a stretcher, and I transferred bodies for other funeral homes and the funeral home of which I worked. It made a little bit of money for me on the side, which would always help a family out raising three children, or parts for my Harley. But, I had a license plate frame that covered the word hearse on the plate and that never stood out using it as a family wagon with the kids bouncing around.

Once I had the kids on a day that there was no school, no work and it afforded us a good snowstorm. We must have gotten 5-6 inches that day, and the kids clamored that they wanted to go to the park! They wanted to play in the snow and go sledding. After repeated requests, I said yes. The kids didn't have one of those fancy metal sleds, and I knew the chance of me finding one at the hardware store was slim to none, so I did what any Father would. I tried to improvise.

I looked around the house and my workshop and could find nothing. With the kids getting louder and louder, I thought for a minute. I then put on a coat and hat, ran out to my station wagon, and popped the back door. There, in a side compartment, rolled up in a plastic wrapper was a green, heavy-duty body bag, as we commonly refer to them. Now, this was no ordinary body bag. In the funeral profession, there is what we usually refer to as a disaster pouch. It is the strongest of the strongest and usually reserved for car accidents, decomps, drownings, crime scenes, and any other messy circumstance that one could imagine.

This heavy green pouch was a durable vinyl, almost the same thickness, but looked like a heavy military-grade pouch. It had cut out handles with a thick wooden dowel encased in the vinyl for an easy carry by whoever was to carry it. Because of the thickness, this thing was heavy. As I removed it from the plastic seal, I almost dropped it twice. The outside was very slick. After placing it on the snow in the front yard, I got a running start and jumped on it. Once I landed on it, my feet went flying out from under me. I busted my ass, and after I regained my stance, my eyes lit up! It was on!

I corralled the three kids, and we made our way to the park. There were many hills, and the place was hopping with activity. Kids of all ages, racing down the several established trails that they had forged. The snow was compacted well, and the temps were right where they needed to be. Not too cold, not too warm.

As I broke out the pouch and we went to the top to await our spot, they were excited, and some people gave us some strange looks. "What is that? That's not a sled. That thing can't be as fast as mine." I felt terrible, and as a father, I wanted to snatch a stranglehold on a few of those little brats, but I let it go.

As our turn came up, I put my oldest two daughters on and wanted to do a trial run. As I grabbed the handles on one end, I curled them around my oldest daughter's legs and feet as she was in the front. I placed the younger daughter's arms around her sister, locking her hands around her waist. I placed the handles in her hand and told her to hold on. I gave a firm shove.

That damn thing took off like a bullet. I went from a skeptic to a nervous wreck as I'm yelling and trying to coach from the top of the hill. Lean-to the right! Lean-to the left! Stay up and in the middle. They were flying! I had no idea that this thing would work, and it did. The girls were screaming so loud I thought, Oh God! I've scared the Hell out of them and ruined them for life. They'll never want to go sledding again."

When I got to the bottom carrying my youngest, I could see that they were not screams of fear, but cries of excitement and they wanted to go again. So, we did. And yet, and again and again. That was the fastest sled on the slopes that day, my friend. I had all three on it at once, and they had a blast. Other kids wanted to try it, and they wanted to trade a ride on theirs for a ride on ours.

Other parents asked me where I got it. Who was the manufacturer? If there were any more like it available for purchase? I just replied, "Oh, I picked it up from a friend. It is a prototype of which he is working. I'm not sure, but I can check.

As we left the park from a full day, the kids were wiped out. I was tired, and I laughed like Hell all the way home. I do every time I think back on that the day and all the fun we had with a body bag. If it works, it's not stupid!

9.

A viewing is usually the time allotted for the family and friends to view the body and to visit and show support for one another. A visitation might not involve the decedent being present, but usually still involves a time for all to gather, grieve and show support.

I have always preferred to work a viewing and, or a visitation as opposed to a funeral ceremony. Visitations were still less formal, more of a meet & greet type of scenario and a time to socialize. But, if I had my druthers, I would prefer to work a Catholic mass as opposed to a Protestant funeral. As a Catholic myself, I knew the order and the Catholic mass like the back of my hand. Stand, sit, stand, sit, stand, sit, stand, kneel, stand, kneel, stand, prayer, recessional. Every time I went through the motions, I would think back to my days in Boot Camp PT in the Army & Coast Guard and laugh!

I was raised in a Protestant family, the grandson of a Baptist minister who converted to Catholicism as an adult. I had worked so many Catholic masses that I fell in love with the beauty of the church, the music, the readings, and scripture, etc. Many times we attend different churches to find one that feels right, and that is how I felt in the Catholic church. It felt right.

At the funeral homes that I worked at, they taught me that as a funeral director; it is our practice to sit on the front row, opposite the family for a Catholic. Not only was it a good idea for the director to be in the church during the mass, but some folks don't go to church as often as they should or know the Catholic Rite. Hence, they could see the director out of the corner of their eye. If they needed to sit, they would see the director sit first. If they needed to stand, they would see the director stand first. And so on. I would sometimes laugh in my head during the movement. I could hear the family following suit, behind my actions, and I thought to myself, "My God! It seems as if we're at Fenway Park and I'm the guy starting The Wave, and everyone is following Me!"

One time, back in the mid-2000s, I was sitting in church, and I had an episode I wished I could erase from my memory, and even happening. I feel worse because it happened in the house of the Lord. I had gone through a divorce in the mid-2000s after a 20-year marriage. I hung around with a close group of guys, and we all rode Harley's. Mostly single guys I moved in with as divorce proceedings took their course. One night we were out later than we should have been. I drank a wee bit more than I probably should have that night. But I got up and carried myself to work.

I had to get into work, as I had a funeral and several things to get in order before. I had only had a few hours of sleep, so I began to load up on caffeine. Back in those days, we always made a car list. I asked everyone that arrived at the funeral home on that morning their relation, their name, and we put them on a car list. When we had to depart the funeral home for the church, we would call our car list. We would start with those that are friends or distant in relation, call them by name, and they would pay their last respects and make their way to their car.

Once everyone was to their cars, we would take the casket to the hearse, load flowers and leave in procession for the church. Once at the church, I would assemble the bearers around the casket. We would follow the priest, processing down the aisle and set the casket in place before the altar. After that point, I would seat the bearers, family, guests, and then have a seat opposite the family. For about the first 20 minutes, I was ok. Then it hit me! I began to feel as if my head weighed a hundred pounds. My eyes got very heavy. I fought as hard as I could. I struggled with all my might, but it beat me. As I felt my head lunge forward, and I am surprised that I did not sustain a concussion from the railing in front of the first pew, or even a whiplash when my head returned to the upright position. I heard it.

I heard the loudest snore I have ever heard in all my life. It was as if someone had let a wild boar loose in the church. With the church in total silence, I lost all control and snored so loud; It woke me up, and I picked my head up in fear! I opened my eyes and looked over at the family, who was staring at me. I let out a few coughs and cleared my throat heavily, trying to mask the whole thing, mouthing in silence "Excuse Me," as I patted my throat and chest.

I then looked upwards to the altar at the priest who was staring at me as he was preparing the gifts before communion. He looked around both raised arms as he held the host in the air, to give me that look that a disapproving parent might give a child. I was so embarrassed and ashamed. The time it took between communion until the recessional hymn seemed like an eternity. Like my soul hung, suspended in time.

After the mass, I made conversation with the priest, telling him I apologized about my coughing attack earlier. He then peered at me, over the rim of his glasses telling me that was ok. It happens, and he would see me on Saturday at confession.

Once out of the church and to the gravesite, I was happy that this funeral was over and in the books. The situation passed. But it took me a long time to live that one down.

One morning we had a funeral scheduled at one of our local Catholic churches. We were all getting ready for the day. We all had the same matching suits for a funeral, and we always kept them in a closet in the main hallway at the funeral home. It was convenient when we went to the dry cleaners to clean our funeral suits, everyone's suit and tie went.

As I was always pulling pranks, this was the perfect opportunity to pull another. Almost every funeral home has at least several sets of glasses, dentures, etc. that they accumulate over the years. Sometimes you will find a drawer in the prep room with such things. On this day or I should say the night before, I had duct-taped a set of upper and lower dentures into my buddy Greg Galanti's suit pants, right inside the crotch.

The next morning we're all getting dressed for a funeral. We were talking about who needs to do what at the church and the score from the Red Sox game the night before. About that time, Greg let out a scream! I'm talking loud. As he dropped his pants in fear, there on the floor, inside his pants, were teeth that looked like an open mouth. To this day, I don't know where he got bit, but I do know that was one of the funniest things I have seen in my life! We laughed and laughed for years over that one and still do.

Once Greg and I came in to make a removal at night. After we did so, I left Greg, excusing myself while he finished logging in the person. At which time, I had taken an old glass eye that I had found in such drawer and gone out and secured it to the dash in his pick-up truck with some black electrical tape.

He came in the next morning, fired up, not happy about how it scared the Hell out of him as he drove home. He said the streetlights passing overhead, had broadcast light downward into his vehicle and it caught his attention as glints of light reflected off it. He said he damn near went off the road trying to figure out why the Hell his dash was winking at him!

Anyway, getting back to the teeth in the pants. After Greg chased me around the funeral home for a few minutes threatening to beat my ass, we all laughed and got back to getting ready. I heard the telephone ring, and I went to answer it as I was the closest. I engaged in the call. I took the information and said that I would have my boss call them back as he was the director that made the arrangements. As I walked out into the hall, one guy says, "What's wrong?" I told my boss he needed to call the family back about the funeral this morning, that they wanted to postpone it. He replied, "Postpone it? They can't postpone it. It's the morning of the funeral." Then I responded that the wife just died not one hour ago, that hospice was there, and we needed to go pick her up. They wanted to do no visitation but wanted to have a mass with both caskets in the church and burial for both at the cemetery.

It took some doing, but we made the removal, made the calls to the church and the cemetery. We sent one of our employees to the Church with the register book so that he could inform those arriving for a funeral Mass that morning, that it would occur the following day, for both husband & wife. That folks were welcome to sign the register if they could not make it the following day.

We already had a casket in stock, and in 24 hours, we had the funeral mass and burial for both. The interesting thing about the passing of both the husband and wife was that they were both hospice patients in hospital beds at home. As it would turn out, both had the same form of cancer according to the doctor's diagnosis. He had been a marine mechanic for many years in the military. During that time, it exposed him to chemicals from years of working on boats. His wife was exposed to it for years from shaking out and laundering his uniforms from work. It was one of the strangest things that I have seen in over 30 years, but in this business, nothing is strange.

Over the road trips always seemed to fall into my lap over the years while I worked on Cape Cod. The Cape was a popular retirement spot for many people from all over the US. Whether it be a local funeral and them burial back in the home city of where people once lived and had a family burial plot, or transport back to their town of origin and all the services there, they had to get there somehow.

I traveled the highways from Cape Cod to Maine, New Hampshire, Vermont, Connecticut, New York, and New Jersey. Beyond that, people would most likely travel via the airlines. The first time I had driven someone to New York City for burial was in the early '90s. It was deep into the downtown parts of the city, one of the oldest cemeteries in the big apple. I can still remember it like it was yesterday.

It was a lovely, expensive hardwood casket. One that I remember that did not leave as frequently as the others because of the price. The visitation and funeral were back on the Cape. I was to drive the gentleman to New York City for burial. There would be no one in attendance at the cemetery. Once I arrived, it would be a burial and a quick turnaround and return. It was about a four and a half-hour drive.

After I arrived, I checked in with the cemetery office; they directed me to where I needed to go, and the cemetery workers met me. They took the casket from the hearse, carried it to the grave and placed it upon the lowering device. The lowering device's purpose is to lower the casket downward into the grave. As it got lower and lower into the grave, I noticed that there was not a vault. A burial vault is a concrete box, with a lid and usually sealed that houses the casket inside the grave. It protects the casket from the weight of the earth and heavy maintenance equipment that will pass over the grave. It also helps resist water and preserves the beauty of the cemetery by preventing the ground from settling.

As the cemetery workers worked to remove the straps from under the casket after lowered, I asked them to stop for a minute. I excused myself for a moment, calling the office and asking my boss if there was to be a vault. He replied that there was not. The cemetery did not require a vault, and the family decided not to spend the money. I returned to the grave and said: "Ok Gentleman, Proceed." With each shovel of earth and rock that hit the shiny, smooth, glossy urethane exterior of that casket, my jaw dropped and my heart. I don't know what a vault sells for in that area, but they were $575 back on the Cape. I would have wanted one if it were one of my family members, but, to each their own. As I drove the hearse out of the cemetery to return to the Cape, I could see many sunken graves, from the result of no vault.

On another road trip, I was once pulled over by a Mass State Police Trooper in our hearse. I was using the HOV lane and informed that the lady in the back was cargo and not a person. I remember saying, "Well, that's rude" and turning my head back towards her and saying, "He didn't mean that Ma'am." He laughed and let me off with a warning.

As stated before, about the liabilities of a deceased individual entrusted into your care, there are many scenarios that any funeral director will tell you it can be a nightmare and sleepless nights.

Whether it be by a malfunctioning refrigeration cooler, a fire at the funeral home, theft of the deceased, etc., it is not a subject anyone in the funeral profession wants to think of or ever face.

Several years ago, I had to drive a gentleman to Newark, New Jersey, to another funeral home. They called and had asked the cost for a remove and embalm, which is where we pick up locally at our end, embalm and secure the paperwork, permit, etc. that we would need to transport out of state. Then they asked what the cost would be to drive them to Newark. They evidently couldn't spare anyone. My boss asked if I wanted to take a road trip and I said I would.

After I hit the road, I met every hazard you could imagine. Traffic, weather, and accidents added hours of delay. I rolled into Newark about 8:30 PM and finally found the funeral home after 9. They stated that no one could come and let me in and that the office would be open again after 8 AM. I began to look around and decided that I would get a room at a motel, get some sleep and be there at 8 AM when they opened. I phoned home and to my boss to let them know what was up and when I expected to be back.

As I looked around for a motel room near the funeral home, the pickings were slim. No wonder they wouldn't send someone out to open the place up. This place gave visualization to the term "seedy." I drove and drove and was still not satisfied with any of the accommodations I spotted. Finally, I picked a motel that was about three miles away, seemed to be in a decent area, and had a fast-food spot nearby and a convenience store.

I drove back to the funeral home, so I knew I could find my way again. I gassed the van up. I grabbed supplies and a few beers at the convenience store and a burger at the restaurant. I returned to the motel, checked in, and got to my room. I parked just outside the door to the motel room, which I felt good about considering I had a body on a stretcher inside.

As I settled in, I made a trip down to the ice machine and returned. I iced down the beer, took a nice hot shower and afterward turned on the television and had a semi-warm burger and a cold beer. I watched a little more tv and finished the second beer before turning in around 11ish. Then about 11:30, it started.

There was a constant traffic flow of people walking up and down the walkway outside. Male voices, female voices, people talking, people laughing, and I'm thinking what in the Hell is going on. I peeked out the curtain, and people were standing in the parking lot and on the corner out by the street. If you want booze, crack or a hooker this was the place you wanted to be, both by the sight and sound of things. I turned the tv back on for a bit, to drown out some sounds. Afterward, it got quiet again, but that didn't last for long. It went back to normal with the activity, people coming and going, etc.

Now, my mind is racing a million miles an hour. Damn! What if they broke into the van? What if they take the body? What if they take the Van and the body? That family would be devastated! That's a million-dollar lawsuit. That funeral home could sue our funeral home. I could lose my job. My kids won't eat. I won't be able to pay my mortgage. We'll be living in a box under an overpass. By that point, I had broken out into a sweat and was on my feet.

I wasn't worried about myself. I've got a concealed carry permit, and I don't go anywhere without it. I carry at work, in churches, on removals, and over the road. My safety was not a concern; It was the deceased of which I worried! I got clothed and went out to the van. I started the engine on the van, backed out of the parking space and backed into the same parking space so that the door was only about four feet away from the door. I locked the van and re-entered the room. I waited and waited. I kept looking out the curtains. As soon as I heard silence, and no one was around, I knew I had to go at that moment.

I hit the key fob, unlocking the van. I quickly looked around, and someone was coming out of a room, so I acted like I was digging around in the cargo area for a few minutes. As soon as they rounded the corner going away from me, I opened the door to my room, jerked the stretcher with the body on it from the van and into my room. I don't even think the wheels had time to hit the walkway between the van and the carpet I acted so quickly. Afterward, I locked the van, locked my door, and pushed the stretcher over to the corner. All I could think about is "Not on my Watch, Your safe tonight, Buddy!"

Now, mind you that there was no way that anyone would steal this gentleman before I can get him to his destination, sleeping with a deceased individual in the same room is not a walk in the park. Oh yeah, I've worked for years in the business and lived, breathed, talked and dealt with death on a multi-faceted level for years! But I've never slept in the same room with a deceased individual. All I could envision was every horror movie that I had seen since childhood and my impending death that people would read about in the newspaper at breakfast in the morning.

I must have opened my eye peaking at that stretcher every five minutes, from 1 AM until my alarm went off at 4 AM! Then I thought about what if something happened to me? What the Hell was that guy doing? Why did he have a dead body in the room with him? That's some "Straight, Jacked Up Serial Killer stuff right there" that you hear about on the internet! I don't think I've ever had more of a sleepless night than I did that night. I set my alarm for 4 AM, thinking "Surely to God by 4 AM, every hooker, crackhead and degenerate in the city should be in bed by then".

I went to the bathroom sink and splashed cold water on my face. I looked out the curtains, nothing. I opened the door and looked to the left and right. I grabbed the key fob and unlocked the van, raised the door, and checked left to right again. Still nothing, so I loaded the stretcher back into the van as quickly as I had emptied it. I took a deep breath; I locked the door, set the alarm for 7 AM, and went back to sleep. I was back at the funeral home by 8 AM to unload and back on the road to the Cape by 8:30. I was exhausted, I turned up the volume to the radio to stay awake, and I drank copious amounts of coffee to make it back home. I'm sure there are some nice sections of Newark. I didn't see them that given night. Nor did I see any I wish to re-visit.

On another instance, years ago, we planned with a family to have a visitation at our funeral home, then the deceased was to be transferred out of state to another funeral home for a visitation and funeral. I was not the director that set it up, because I would have never allowed the timing between the two functions or venues. The morning after a viewing at our location, the transport company that we use sent a driver to our facility for pick up. I had everything ready. The casket was closed. The decedent was positioned accordingly with plastic and cotton around the head and under the hands. This was to prevent any risk of hands or cosmetics to soil the clothing. I would usually do this with a flight or over the road transportation.

The young lady that arrived introduced herself, and I remarked that I had never met her before. She stated that she was new and had worked with the owner in another capacity years ago. Once loaded into the van, I handed her the paperwork that had the permit for the other funeral home. She also had the address and phone number. She had an itinerary of the visitation time, and I told the funeral time to call them at a specific time to let them know how far she was at that point.

I had a visitation that morning, which began around 11 AM, with a funeral starting at noon. I had greeted the family when they arrived at 10, gotten them in and settled and was working the front door and having people sign the guest register, etc. Right around 11:45 AM, our receptionist called me over for an incoming phone call. As I answered, I stated that this was Kevin. Can I help you? The female voice at the other end of the line indicated that her name was Corporal Thomas, with the Florida State Police and she asked if we were transporting a body out of state and if we were she needed to discuss that with me.

My first impression was that one of my coworkers was messing with me. I liked a prank as much as the next person, and someone was having fun at my expense. My response was ok, Ha, Ha, who is this, and where did you get your info.? As I heard silence at the other end, she stated that she was serious, this was no joke, and she noted the deceased individual's name and the driver's name. At that point, I knew it was not a joke.

It is 11:50, and I had a family to go to the casket one more time before we closed it, a minister to corral to the lectern, a family to seat and service to begin. I then asked to place her on hold so I could get someone to assist her. I then asked the receptionist to get the boss, so he could take care of it. What I had going on was time-sensitive, not that this wasn't, but as any funeral director will tell you. When it's time for the service to begin, it's time for the service to start. I had a full order of service to follow. I was running the sound, music, and the announcement afterward to leave for the cemetery.

After I returned from the cemetery and could sit down to understand it finally, it is as follows.

At around 75 miles per hour, the driver suffered a blowout of the front left tire. The blow out resulted in the van going off the road and into the grassy median. It was at this point that it had ripped the wheel off the vehicle. The accident resulted in the casket getting shaken all over the inside of the van. So, going from the description of a trooper, we do not know if there is damage to the casket, nor the individual inside.

We contacted the livery service that we use and he contacted another livery service in that area who could get right over to the scene as quickly as possible. Again, it's another individual giving us an assessment that to the best of their knowledge and ability, they cannot see any damage to the casket. We called the other funeral home to tell them what has happened and assured them we would get the individual there as quickly as possible. We called the family and informed them as to things. It just so happened they drove by the disabled vehicle right after it happened, not knowing that it was their family member inside.

As the visitation hour neared, the other funeral home was calling several times for an update. We called the driver to get a status on where they were. Minutes seemed like hours and hours seemed like days as we would wait for an update whether the driver had made it to the destination yet. The family was at the other funeral home, and guests were arriving. The visitation was to begin at 4 PM. We received a call from the funeral home that the driver had arrived; the casket was fine and had suffered no damage in the accident, nor had the deceased, other than having to touch up the cosmetics. They wheeled the casket into their chapel area and in place at 3:55 and they opened the doors for the visitation to begin.

There is an old saying, "As nervous as a Dog pooping over a briar patch." That was us on that given day. Not necessarily that the accident was anyone's fault, but planning could have been a little better to allow a cushion, and when something goes wrong, it can affect everyone involved.

In 30 years as a funeral director, I have had to officiate the committal prayers at a cemetery several times because of a priest or clergy that had gotten lost trying to find the grave or that they had been involved in an auto accident, etc.

I've often equated being a funeral director to an actor. You are there to do a job. If something goes wrong, you deal with it. You don't get excited. You don't make a scene, and you don't show nervousness. If you do, that is when other people see it, and it appears as if something is wrong. Just roll with the punches.

Several years ago, I had a family come into the funeral home and planning a funeral for their father. We made all the arrangements, and they informed me that one son was building a casket. Whenever I hear those words, my mind goes crazy, especially after this instance. I often wonder about the quality of said casket and its structural integrity. Since then, I have always required the family to sign a third-party merchandise waiver, stating that the funeral home, nor its employees are responsible for any issues, defects or faults with the said casket. If it comes from somewhere other than us, we're not responsible for its quality.

A day before the visitation, they had delivered the casket. The appearance impressed me. It was a beautiful poplar casket, with a cherry stain and a sleek, shiny urethane coat. The hardware was a little different from what we are used to seeing on other caskets, and it was very nicely constructed. As I had gotten the gentleman ready for his visitation, I opened the casket and placed him inside. I positioned him accordingly and got the pillow just right, as well as his hands.

I set him up in our chapel area. The family arrived shortly after that, and the visitation had begun. The attendance was excellent; the family was grieving appropriately and talking, laughing, and telling stories. I had heard several people say to others that the son had made the casket. They all raved about the detail and work that he had put into it. It turned out that Dad enjoyed woodworking, and this was one last thing that the son could do for him. I admired that.

The following morning we met at the family's church. Right before the service, I assembled the pallbearers, led them to the hearse, and we carried the casket into the church. It was a lovely service and attended by many. Afterward, we brought the casket back out to the hearse and made our way to the cemetery.

Upon reaching the cemetery and everyone exiting their vehicles, I assembled the bearers one last time. We removed the casket from the hearse. We turned, so we were leading with the foot end of the casket. We made our way to the grave with the family a little behind us. It would appear as it was taking the wife a little longer to make her way to the grave, so the kids said to set the casket in place and informed them I would come back to walk her over.

As we made our way to the grave, I heard the unsettling sounds. It was several creaks, followed by a ripping sound and then a thud. As the deceased came crashing out of the bottom of that casket and to the ground, so didn't my heart! Oh my God, I thought. And, with the bottom of the casket lying there on earth, so wasn't their husband and father. Still, on the pillow, hands even folded one on top of the other and not a stitch of clothing torn.

I was in shock, but more so were the pallbearers. They just froze. As I quietly muttered, "Put it down. Put it down. Put it down"! Each time getting louder than the last, I finally reached out and physically pushed the casket down on top of and around the gentleman. I then told them to leave it there. I quickly tucked whatever casket interior in and under as best as I could.

About that time, the family came walking up. Thank God a row of monuments had blocked their view of the incident. The son who had built the casket was a pallbearer. I leaned over to him and said that if he wanted to tell his mother that the grave was having cave-in issues and the cemetery wants us to do the committal here, I would go along with it. We were merely 20 feet from the grave.

He did, and that message quickly got relayed to most of the attendees. Once everyone dispersed, they finally told her that the bottom had let go. She questioned what they meant, let out a laugh and said that's your Dad, being difficult right until the damn end! Everyone laughed and felt a little more at ease over the incident.

I told them they were ok to watch if they wished, but that we would slide a few nylon straps under the casket, pick it up and carry it over to the lowering device and take it from there. They stayed and watched right until they placed the vault lid.

Several years later, the wife had died. As we were making the arrangements, other children turned to the son and asked him if he would build another casket for the mom. He stated no that his casket building days were over and if one of them would like to, he would be sure to bring extra screws for the bottom.

Many times, we as funeral directors see that people want a service to be different. They want original and not the same old "cookie-cutter" type of ceremony that they had experienced before. We've done everything to parking a guy's favorite sports car or Harley next to the casket, to a custom, flamed paint job on a casket to anything imaginable.

At one funeral several years ago, we had a visitation the night before the funeral. We had a fair amount of flowers and visitors for the family that evening. The next morning, we lowered the flowers on the flower stands to where they needed to be with the casket closed. We placed the lectern into the room for the Pastor to use, and we removed the casket, leaving a big vacant area in the middle of all the flowers. We vacuumed and got ready for the funeral.

As people began to arrive, we asked them to sign the guest register if they had not the previous evening and ushered people in to take their seats. It was funny as people whispered to those around them. They were asking about a missing casket. What was going on was the funeral here? As the service time grew near, we ushered the family in, seated them, and the Pastor entered. We closed the doors, and he began the funeral. As I peered in from a back door, I could still see the bewilderment on people's faces.

After the greeting and introduction by the Pastor, he had a seat, and we played the first song. As the song concluded, two of the funeral home associates opened the double doors, wheeled the casket into place, turned to the casket in unison, slightly bowed and departed the room together. Again, the look on everyone's face was precious.

As the Pastor stood, approached the lectern and stated to those in attendance, "I am sure there are those of you who are wondering what has just transpired here? And, I am sure there are those of you present, who could honestly say, If you knew Bill, then you would know that he would probably be late for his own funeral".

The place erupted in laughter! The family was in hysterics and the guests. This was what the family wanted and what Bill would have loved. We had more people commenting afterward upon leaving how tickled they had gotten over that scenario and how fitting it was for Bill.

We did that same scenario with another funeral; only this time it was a gentleman who was in sales. He was always on his phone. He was always taking sales orders, trying to make a sale or following up to the delivery of a sale. I mean, always on the phone.

They gave us his cell phone number, and we placed his phone behind the casket. The Pastor had instructed us that after about five minutes to call his number. When we did, we were to allow it to ring for about five times. And we were to repeat it one minute after that. And then to repeat it, about one minute after that. After the first two times, he looked around chastising whoever would bring their phone to a funeral and not silence it or turn it off. Upon the third call, the Pastor had followed the sound to behind the casket, picked up the phone and said, "I should have known without a doubt, that it was Gene." Picking up the phone for everyone to see. And, and the crowd laughed, for that was Gene.

Anything you can do to make that ceremony memorable and fitting of that person or their family is what sets a funeral home apart from others.

You often have religious services and secular services, and you have to know how to differentiate between the two. I have usually commented that one of the hardest jobs in the death care profession is that of a hospice chaplain. They come in to offer guidance to a family at one of the worst times of their life, and they usually have to be walking on eggshells when doing so.

You can't just walk into a room and start talking about God, religion, and the hereafter to someone if you don't understand their beliefs or spirituality. They and other workers in the field deal with sorrow, depression, and anger. And frankly, it can get directed at anyone in this field.

Several times I have dealt with anger from a family over the circumstances of a death. Not that they had any reason to be angry at me, but they were looking for someone to take it out on. Which brings to mind a certain gentleman.

Tony, as I will refer to him as he came into our office one day asking about services and prices and stating that his son was on state assistance. I informed him of what was allowable under the state assistance program and answered his questions. He told me that was not what he wanted. He wanted two visitations on the same day, a funeral the following day at the church burial at a specific cemetery and a limousine.

Each time this man opened his mouth, he got ruder and even more hateful. I added up the figures for what he had requested and given him the total. By this point, I was feeling pushed to where I had enough. He then stated to me he would make some price comparison, which I thoroughly encouraged him to do. As I was walking him to the door, his words to me were, "You're not the only funeral home in town." I turned to him and said, "No Sir, we are not, but we are the most reasonably priced. When you want to re-group and finish arranging your son's services, call me." He then shot me a nasty stare.

That night about 8 PM, I received a call from the answering service that Tony was calling and wanted to use our services for his son. He stated that he wanted me to call him. I did, and he was adamant that I met him at the funeral home at night to finish the arrangements. He seemed put out and not understanding that I would not. He repeatedly pushed, and I finally told him NO. It was 8 PM; I was at home with my family, and I would set an appointment for the following morning for 10 AM.

The next morning upon his arrival, we set everything in motion, just as he requested. Not according to the state-assisted plan, but with the two visitations, funeral, burial and limousine.

At the visitation, I met Tony's wife, son, daughter-in-law, and two granddaughters. They all seemed like a beautiful family, but you could see that Tony was the patriarch of the family, what he said or did was the Gospel and no one bucked him! Even after the visitation he sat with his son and refused to go home between 4-7 PM. At 9 PM, I went into the room and discussed what time the limo would be there to pick the family up at their home and walked them to the door.

The next morning, we had two funeral masses at two different Catholic churches. We could not leave the building at the same time with two different funerals and families, so it was our practice that we offset the mass times by one hour. After one family and procession was out the door, we were situated and ready to expect the next family. After the first family was getting ready to leave, the phone rang. It was my limo driver telling me that there was an accident blocking his route to the family home. While he was on one line, I had to pause that call and answer the other line.

On the other line was a very upset, Tony, asking me where the limo was. Telling me he should have been at the funeral home an hour ago so he could sit with his son. As I refreshed his memory about what we discussed the previous night, his volume increased and his temper. He finally hung up on me, and I resumed my call with the limo driver. I asked the driver where he was; I thought for a moment, then I detoured him and alternately guided him. Once I knew he was on the correct street, I finished the call. I then called the family's home and let them know the car was on their road, at which point Tony yelled and hung up on me again.

As I waited at the front door for the limo to arrive, I was going over everything in my head. Which flowers were to go into the church for the mass, both granddaughters were to bring up the gifts for the Eucharist, etc.

As I watched the limousine pull into the parking lot and up to the front of the building, I could see the rear door burst open before the car came to a complete stop. When it did, I saw Tony emerge from the rear and make a beeline to me at the front door of the funeral home. He immediately got into my face telling me that the limo was late (which it was by only 5 minutes because of the accident) that he should have been here an hour ago so he could sit with his son. By this point, I had hit Mount St. Helens mode and was ready to erupt!

As I looked him in the eye, I said, "Look, Mr. Scarpacci. I've had just about enough of this. I don't get paid enough to put up with your shit, and I will not continue to put up with your shit. The car was at your home at the designated time that we discussed last evening. If you had wanted to be here earlier, you should have stated that. Now, I suggest that you spend what time we have with your son before I have to dismiss everyone to the church for the Mass,".

At that point, I felt shocked that I had uttered those words to this man. But I also felt as if someone had lifted the weight of the World off my shoulders. As he growled at me, walking past me to gain entry to be with his son, his wife walked up to me, grabbed my hand, and squeezed it. The son winked at me, while his wife silently mouthed, "Thank You." The two granddaughters just looked at me as to say, welcome to our world.

At the designated time, I entered and announced that we would need to leave to make the church on time. I invited them to go to the casket one more time and if they would like me to close it in their presence. They chose to be there for the closing, I did, and we walked out together. As I walked the family out to the limo, Tony grabbed my arm, shook my hand, and said: "We're still friends." I felt a little more at ease after the words and tone I had taken with Tony. We concluded the mass, went to the cemetery, and the family again☐ thanked me after I walked them to the limousine to leave.

Several months later, I was at the cemetery conducting a graveside service, and I saw Tony visiting his son's grave. I mentioned it to the superintendent, and he remarked that Tony was out there daily. And☐ he would come into the office almost daily, to complain why there were no porta-potties at the cemetery. And the superintendent would threaten him practically daily that if he caught him urinating on the cemetery property again that he would call the police. Months after that, as I suspected, they had diagnosed Tony with Alzheimer's disease. I had a feeling he was exhibiting signs from our initial encounter with one another.

One day, I received a call from the son that Tony had died. I met with both he and Mrs. Scarpacci to arrange the visitation and mass. It was almost an exact duplicate of what we had done before. A few days later, I got him ready, dressed and in his casket, I placed him in the chapel area and waited for his family to arrive. I checked him over one more time under the overhead lighting, making sure his shirt, tie, and suit were just right. I took a lint roller and touched up his jacket.

As I did, I reminisced about the day of his son's funeral, and I laughed at the memory of him busting that limo door open, it almost coming off the hinges and him getting in my face. As I adjusted the knot on his tie and centered it on his collar, I said, "We're still friends Tony, we're still friends."

12.

After over thirty years in the business, there are still things that never cease to amaze me. Occasionally we would have a biker funeral. I'm not talking about a group of guys that get together on a Saturday and ride down to the Harley shop and out to eat afterward. I'm talking about one percenter motorcycle clubs that have been around since the '40s. Guys that look like they would take you out back and never to be seen or heard from again.

We would work out the details with the arrangements. As usual, they paid the bill in cash, and sometimes we were to order the casket and once delivered, we were to call the club to come to pick it up. They would return the casket with some of the most impressive paint schemes and flame jobs that you have ever seen. Almost a shame to place it in the ground

Often for these types of visitations, we would see an unmarked police cruiser parked across the street and the reflection of a telephoto camera lens as photo after photo was taken. You would see guys riding in with bandanas over their faces to conceal their identity and then lowered once they were inside the confines of our building. They would visit with the family for a while and other members, then once going out the door, back up with the bandana.

Out of respect for the parents of the deceased things were mostly low key, but after they departed and it was just club members, spouses, and girlfriends, it could go into a full-blown party mode. Sometimes after everyone left, we were cleaning and removing empty bottles of whiskey from the wastebaskets and a few empty beer cans from the outside shrubs. But, mostly, we only a few instances where something had gotten broken, and they were happy to cover it.

On the day of the funeral, we always had a large attendance of members on their bikes. The roar of Harley's could be heard from blocks away as we approached in procession. They blocked intersections as we made our way through and on our way to the church. If we were not going to a church, then as we made our way to the cemetery. Sometimes it was just to the cemetery for a graveside service. If it was a church service, occasionally we might have to approach several members and ask them to remove a hat while in church, which they were always cooperative and respectful of that request.

After the church, it was off to the cemetery. Often clubs would have the monument or tombstone delivered early. That way, it was on display the day of the burial. Frequently, the club would have a representative camp out overnight to guard the grave and monument.

Once at the cemetery, the members carried the casket to the grave and placed it upon the lowering device. After the priest or pastor completed the committal ceremony and the parents if any left, it was back into Party Mode. I always told us to have at least six to eight shovels on hand for the club to use at the grave. A big galvanized tub of iced down beers would come out, and it would begin. If the club wanted to put the vault lid on by hand, we extended them that opportunity, and we always had chains and straps on hand if that was the case. Sometimes they would allow the vault company to use machinery for placement of the lid. But after that, it was all by hand.

They would have two to four guys each place about ten shovels of earth onto the top of the vault. Then they would hand off the shovels, crack a beer, kill it and get back in line to help close the grave. They were always pouring beer into the grave for the departed brother. It was impressive to see, and they didn't stop until they had filled the grave. Once slightly higher, they would stop as they knew the vault company would have to tamp it and re-sod, etc.

Afterward, you could hear the roar of the Harley's and off to the reception or party later. It was pretty much just let them do their thing and stay out of their way.

There was an instance once where I had to stay back once they left for the church. I believe I had another person to dress and casket for an afternoon ceremony. For some reason, I can't recall why we had kept the register book and printed materials back. But the doorbell rang at the front door, and I answered it. It was a detective from the local PD. He had asked if we still had the register book or had it gone to the church. I stated that we did. He asked if he could see it. When I asked him if he had a warrant, he said no, but he could get one. I then responded that I would have to see a warrant before I was to release anything. I went about my business, and he never returned.

Another dilemma that a funeral director can face is forgetting a very important detail. Such as something that should have been removed before closing the casket and departing for the cemetery. Sometimes it can be something simple, and in other instances, it could be a valuable piece of jewelry or a family heirloom. One trick I began to use was to pin a post-it note under the extendover. The extendover is a part of the casket upholstery which folds over and downward to hide the edge of the casket where the hinged top folds down and makes contact with the casket side.

This way the note would not be visible by the public but would be right in my face, upon closing of the casket, to make sure I did not forget to do something I was supposed to. I began using that method after the following story.

Every so often, you run across a family that you love to work with. You hate the fact that they need your services, but if they do, you want to be the one that they call, and you want to be the best that you can be. I can honestly say that it is one of the most significant rewards in the funeral business.

This specific family was one of those families. The wife had passed, and I was working with the husband and the daughters on the arrangements and funeral. The husband was a remarkably friendly and down-to-earth guy. The daughters were absolute sweethearts. When they came in, they knew how they wanted things to be. From the visitation, what music they wanted at the funeral. They knew how they wanted Mom, and her appearance, in what clothing, what pictures for the DVD, and they had even written the obituary. All I needed to do was to put it all together.

I did. When the family comes in to see their loved one for the first time can be one of the most nervous times for any funeral director. They began crying loudly. I peeked in to make sure everyone was ok and as I did; They went from crying to talk to laughing, and I knew all was well. After a few minutes, I walked in to see if they needed me to make any adjustments or corrections. When I did, they stated how beautiful Mom looked, how pleased they were and that they only had one request. They wanted me to place a ring on her finger.

They brought in her wedding band and her mother's ring with the clothing, but they said that this was another ring that had a very significant meaning. This ring was her great, great grandmother's ring. It was centuries old and had come over on the boat, on her finger, from Europe when she did. I examined it and admired it for a few minutes, placed it on her finger, and then asked if there was anything else that I could do or be of further help. I alerted them where the restrooms were and stated that I would be working at the front door, should they need anything.

The attendance for the visitation was good. There were many people from the village and the surrounding community. There was also a fair amount of folks that drove down from Boston, who were coworkers of the daughters- and sons-in-law. I seem to remember the visitation ending at 9 PM, but most people didn't leave and give the family their last private time until at least 9:45.

As I arrived the following morning, I washed both the station wagon for flowers and the hearse. We vacuumed and prepped the funeral home for the service and set up chairs. I ran down my to-do list and had everything set. I had the location for the reception afterward on an index card, in my jacket pocket. I would keep repeating it to recite at the end of the committal at the cemetery.

As the family arrival time neared, I gave her a final inspection in the casket, in case I needed to make any corrections and I then waited out in front of the funeral home for them to arrive. It was a beautiful day, and I enjoyed the fresh air. As they pulled in, I waived them to park right in the front of the funeral home, which would put the five cars right in line to follow the hearse upon departure to the cemetery. I walked them in and let them know that I would be around if they needed anything. I would keep an eye out for the Pastor and bring him in when he arrived.

After the Pastor arrived, I brought him in to talk with the family. As it got to be ten minutes before the service, I asked the family if they would like to approach the casket once more before closing it for the service. They did, and after I walked the last one to their seat, I approached the casket. I carefully slid off the wedding band and the mother's ring and placed them in my pocket. I would later put them into a velvet jewelry bag that we customarily returned the jewelry to the family in.

As I reached for the third ring, I heard a loud noise behind me. I turned, and one daughter had tripped and fallen on the floor. I'm not sure what she was doing if she was trying to approach the casket again, but I quickly turned and got to her to lend aid. I got her to her feet, as did a few other family members and she made her way to her chair. I asked if she was all right; She stated that she was, and I went back to the casket where I slowly tucked in the interior and gently closed the lid, slowly, as is our practice. As I excused myself, I closed the chapel doors and went to man the music.

After the service, I entered the chapel and announced that we would depart to the cemetery. That everyone should travel with headlights and hazard lights on, and if everyone would kindly adjourn to their vehicles. Once everyone was out to their cars, we removed floral cards, loaded the flowers, and had taken the casket to the hearse. Once the flowers were on their way, we circled to the front, had the family file in behind the hearse and made our way to the cemetery which was only a few miles away.

Once at the cemetery, the pallbearers carried the casket to the grave, as I led the family behind. After the family and friends assembled, the Pastor began the committal Service. After the prayers, I made my recitation about the gathering at a local restaurant that the family had arranged. As I walked the family to their vehicles, they thanked me, said how beautiful everything was and how happy they were. After they had placed the lid on the vault, we made our way back to the funeral home.

We all jumped in and began cleaning up, removing, folding, and stacking the chairs. Putting the rooms back together in an informal visitation style floor plan and cleaning things up. After a short while, the phone rang, and one of the guys told me to pick up. As I picked up, it was the husband from the funeral we had just completed. He stated that he checked the bag with the register book, pamphlets and floral cards and that he did not find the rings. I told him that in confusion and when his daughter had fallen; I had them in my pocket and did not put them in yet. He stated that it was all right. He would spend time with his family and guests and retrieve them in the morning at the funeral home.

As I completed our conversation, I replaced the handset onto the phone, and I reached into my pocket to retrieve the three rings. There was only one problem. There were only two rings in my pocket. As I withdrew the two rings, my jaw dropped, and my heart. Where was the other ring? Had it fallen out of my pocket? I quickly ran downstairs to the garage to check the hearse. I checked the seat and the floorboards. No ring. I ran into the chapel and checked the floor near where the casket was. No ring. By this point, my boss is asking me what I am doing, and I just made off like I was looking for my keys.

After checking a few more places, and the hearse again, it hit me. I had removed two rings. As I went for the third ring, that was when the daughter had fallen. I went to assist her in her seat. I had forgotten about the third ring. I closed the casket. The ring is still in the casket. Oh Shit!

I quickly ran downstairs to the prep room for a little privacy and called the cemetery. As the phone began to ring, I kept telling myself in my head. Maybe they went to lunch after the top went onto the grave liner. Perhaps they're just now getting to backfill the grave. By this point, I was sweating profusely, and I was sick to my stomach. The cemetery superintendent answered, and I asked him if the grounds crew had closed the grave yet. He stated that they had. As I let out a few select curse words, he asked why, and the only thing I could come up with was that my keys were missing, and I wondered if anyone had found them. He stated that they had not, but he would keep an eye out.

As I hung up the phone, my heart once again sank. I was sick and ready to pass out. Being a younger married couple with three children, I could not afford to pay the opening fee to have the cemetery re-open the grave. And, if my boss had to pay for that, he would not be happy. I thought long and hard all day on what my next move was. I thought about every scenario. I tried to figure a way out to get that ring back with no one knowing, and I thought about how to do it with the least amount of people knowing.

As 5 pm rolled around, we all went our separate ways at the end of the workday. The next morning, the husband showed up to retrieve the three rings, which I had neatly placed into the usual velvet jewelry bag. He removed them, began to tear up, put them back into the bag, and thanked me for everything. He told me how pleased he and his family were with our services. I thanked him for those words and said if he needed anything else, please let me know. I grimaced a little as he gave me a tight handshake as my hands were a bit chafed and tender. I walked him out to his car, and when I returned, I sat down, let out a deep breath and said: "Thank you, Jesus."

I will neither confirm nor deny the details of what I did to get that ring back, but you can bet your sweet ass I got it back! I will say that I was running on very little sleep the next day and living on coffee until bedtime that night. I've never been more relieved in my life than the moment I could place those three rings in that man's hand!

One of the few things that I have never really come to understand over the years is suicide. I can somewhat understand and relate in an instance of euthanasia when someone is terminally ill, undergone treatment, and tired from the long ordeal with no hope in sight. But I've never really understood it from an aspect of just wanting to leave this life. An old friend and mentor once said it was explained to him earlier that suicide is a permanent solution to a temporary problem. And to me, there has never been a more accurate definition over the years.

When I worked at a funeral home that had the contract for the two local Air Force bases, I was often tasked with the duties of getting these young servicemen embalmed and prepared.

It was a task I dreaded and often a pain in the backside and I say this with the utmost respect as I served proudly in both the US Army and the US Coast Guard, and years in each.

I felt proud to care for these young men and women. However, most people know how the US Military does things, and frankly, and most often, those measures or means aren't always the most sensible. There is always a rigid amount of inspections of the deceased before you're allowed to begin the process. Often it is a very detailed, time-consuming, and tedious process. On more than several occasions, I have made the statement that the active-duty contract has much room for improvement and has downfalls, making one regretful for even bidding on it.

In most instances, a Government Contractor is working as a liaison with that branch of the military. They are usually in charge of reporting to and working with the family. I have always commented, "Do your inspection, converse on your own time and call us when we can come in and embalm, patchwork and let us do our jobs."

Most overseas and KIA, or killed in action deaths for any military personnel, are cared for by the US Military Mortuary Affairs team at Dover AFB. Mostly, any time a funeral home here in the states cares for an active-duty person, it is because death happened stateside. Yes, most of the ones I had the privilege to care for were just regular kids living their lives, being adventurous, and there were the suicides. And I have always looked at the suicides and reflected on what my Buddy used to say, suicide is a permanent solution to a temporary problem.

Usually, the suicides of the young active-duty men or women were over something most would view as trivial — relationship issues, family problems, etc. And then the old verbiage of a permanent solution to a temporary problem would scroll back through my mind.

I once requested the local Mortuary Affairs team at the two local Air Force Bases, to please bring us white gloves, typically used for dress uniforms. They thought the request was odd and questioned my purpose. I reminded them that many of the cases we get are accidents, etc. We live in a coastal community, and we get many drownings, boating accidents, motorcycle accidents, etc.

Often I would have to dry out the hands and use our surgical gloves as a protective barrier to prevent leaks and apply the white dress gloves to hide the surgical gloves. It also helped to keep cosmetics off the uniforms. Once they came around to my way of thinking, they made it usual practice after that. Not to mention, it looked sharp.

Whether it be an active duty death or a veteran who has passed, I will always find time to iron and press a US flag. One of my biggest pet peeves is never to have a wrinkled flag on a casket. I have a large oversized pool table in my home, which I can drape a flag over and an ironing board at the end. It makes an ideal station to press a flag. Once pressed, I can then drape over a large hanger and readily take to work the next morning. I find satisfaction in knowing I can do this simple task for any honorably discharged veteran. I'd feel honored for someone to do it for me someday.

Back on Cape Cod, we had a gentleman that owned a dry cleaning business in Centerville that we took all of our US flags to be pressed. The owner spoke with a heavy European accent. I asked one day why no charge for the funeral home when he pressed a flag. He turned to me and stated, "Because I know what the flag represents, and I know where each of the flags is going. I immigrated to this country with my family years ago. I wanted a better life for them and myself. I find great honor in being able to press a flag for anyone who has served their country.

Any funeral director will tell you they have encountered their share of suicides over the years. They come in many modes, manners, and circumstances. It's often said that when a woman commits suicide, she is usually very neat about it. And when a male commits suicide, it is just the opposite. After witnessing both, I would have to agree with that rationale.

I had a gentleman walk in one day to make pre-arrangements. I had no other appointments, so I sat down with him. We went over different options. He chose what he wanted and even paid for it. He was upbeat and talked about his family and grandchildren. He never let on like anything was bothering him.

The next afternoon I read the story about a man who had driven to the Sheriff's Office in the next county, called the dispatch desk, and told them that there was a dead body, and they needed to call the medical examiner's office. When the dispatch operator asked for the address so that they could send a deputy, he said in your parking lot. It was at that instance that the operator heard a loud pop, placed the phone on to the counter, walked over, looked out in the parking lot, and saw the red spray all over the windows of the parked car. When they published the name, I remembered it as being the gentleman in question. He conveniently placed his pre-arrangement paperwork in a Ziploc bag, on the passenger seat, so that they knew who to call after the medical examiner had finished.

One day I had a guy call the funeral home threatening to commit suicide, but on this day, I had the opportunity to prevent it. I hope the decision I made helped this gentleman out. I often wonder if it did.

Our receptionist received a call one morning from a gentleman that stated he needed our services. She asked him if there was a death, or if this was for someone who had not yet passed. He noted that it was for him, but that by the time we arrived, he would have already passed. After our receptionist heard that, she alerted another employee who came and got me. As I approached, I could listen to some of the conversation, and the other employee informed me of the rest of the dialogue.

I quickly grabbed my laptop, returned to the front office, and started plugging in data so that I could gain more info on the man. I ran his name in our system and could not see that we had buried anyone in his family. I then ran his name in the local tax collector's office and came up with an address. I asked the receptionist to get his phone number, in case they got disconnected.

With his name and number, and knowing in what jurisdiction he lived, I called the sheriff's office, gave them the info, details and within 4 minutes, our receptionist said that there was a knock at the door. The gentleman stated that he had to answer the door, and she would need to hold on, as he placed the phone on the counter.

As the gentleman answered the door, she could hear the deputy come in, speak to the man in question. The deputy then picked up the phone, telling her they were on the scene and everything was ok. They would help him and contacting someone from his family to come over and check on him. I often wonder if what I did was the right thing to do, but at that moment, it felt right.

Years ago, we had what looked like a suicide, but the medical examiner ruled it an accidental death. He called it autoerotic asphyxiation. It was back in the early '90s when I witnessed my first autoerotic asphyxiation death. They called us to the scene to pick up for the local Medical Examiner. The guy was a local CPA, and one of his buddies had shown up to pick him up as they were going out on the town for the night. The friend arrived at the designated time. There was no answer to the door. He thought he was running late, still in the shower, etc. He walked around the house to bang on the bedroom window and received no answer.

As he made his way back around the house, he looked in a window and noticed his friend hanging from a hook in the ceiling by a rope, feet on the floor and knees bent. He called the police who arrived and gained entry. Once inside, the police discovered porn playing on the television. They also found a lime wedge on the floor in front of him.

The scene was cleared, and the wedge tagged and bagged. I asked the Medical Examiner what the significance was of the lime wedge and reasoning why this was an accidental death. Not knowing much about autoerotic asphyxiation he tried to explain it to me. He stated, "You've experienced an orgasm during sex, correct? "Of course", I said. "Imagine an orgasm ten times that intense! That's what happens when you rob your brain of oxygen at the same instance of orgasm. It's an epidemic, and it's killing hundreds of young people a year."

"The Lime," he said, "is a way to shock the senses back and to regain consciousness. The citrus acid works muck like ammonia inhalants when someone has fainted. Only it fell out of the mouth. Without that citric acid to do its job to revive the person, it was, in turn, an accidental death."

Over the years, we saw more and more of the autoerotic asphyxiation. Young people, older people, and famous people. Not just autoerotic asphyxiation, but also suicides and from some of those who claim to have suffered from depression. People from all walks of life, all backgrounds. I often wondered why?

Depression affects many people and more than we think. As hard as I search, I really can't find an answer. Many times we look at someone and think, "What the Hell reason could this person possibly have to be unhappy or depressed? They've got the world at their fingertips and disposal. It makes little sense.

Is life that difficult? Is it that hard to find a happy place? Some things will always remain a mystery. It will still leave some things unsaid, as any funeral director will tell you.

Another term about suicide that conveys a strong message is that suicide doesn't take the pain away. It passes it to someone else.

For years I've looked into the eyes of family members who have lost a loved one and had huge chunks ripped from their hearts. I've looked through their tears into their hollow eyes and held their hands. I've tried to offer some comforting words. Many funeral directors have been in the same situation.

It's easier to find the words when it is an older person who dies naturally or when it is an expected death. But when it is a suicide, it leaves so many questions and confusion for the survivors. Could I have been there more? Could I have listened more? Too many what if's?

Sometimes there are no words that will genuinely bring solace. Sometimes all you can do is try your hardest to make their experience a little better considering the circumstances. As a funeral director, I may not be able to fill the void from their loss but, if I can do anything in my power to ease their pain, I will. If I can attempt to make their loved one more presentable for viewing, I will. I'll give it my best. Sometimes that means more than any words of comfort that I could facilitate.

Laughter is sometimes the best medicine. If you can take a family that is going through a difficult time and give them the least bit of levity, or a moment to laugh, you have given them something more valuable than earthly possessions. I always attempt to listen to a family talk. Sometimes it is a split second, sometimes off the cuff, but at some point, there is usually an opportunity to inject a least little of levity or a chance to make them smile.

I once had two women that came in and planned the funeral of their sister who had died. They were career gals who retired from Boston to the Cape. One was a secretary for an attorney, and the two surviving sisters retired from the electric company and the other from the public school system. All three had never married, retired within five years of one another, and lived in three homes next to one another on the same street.

They were a Hoot. As I sat with them and we discussed the arrangements they wished for their sister, they said that the funeral mass was to be local, but the burial would be in the family plot in Boston. I heard stories of their childhood, growing up, and that the three of them were the closest in the family and had been over the years. When they remarked that they were the last three of fourteen children, I commented, "Wow, your parents must not have had a television when they got married" They laughed and laughed at that one.

That was the beginning of a long-lasting friendship. Over the next few years, Mary and Eileen would call and stop by the funeral home with fresh-baked cookies in arms, and I would run across the street to get us coffee at the Dunkin Donuts. They had nieces and nephews back in Boston, but I think maybe I filled that void of not having any locally. They both set an appointment to come in and make pre-arrangements for themselves and wanted everything just the way it was for Susan, the sister I had previously buried.

There was to be a visitation at the funeral home. The following day would comprise a funeral mass at their church. Later, we would meet at the cemetery in Boston at a designated time for the committal, and there was to be no sedan for the family. The surviving sister was to ride with me from the Cape to Boston in the hearse.

One day I received the call that Mary had passed. I made the arrangements, and we did it just the way they wanted. It was a lovely funeral mass and attended by nieces and nephews from Boston, and neighbors and parishioners from the church. Upon Eileen's insistence, I sat with her instead of opposite the family as I usually do for a Catholic mass. Once the pallbearers placed the casket into the hearse, I announced that we would all meet at the cemetery for the committal. I loaded the flowers, packed up the register book and printed material, and seated Eileen in the front of the hearse.

I was a little taken back when asked to stop at the Dunkin Donuts after leaving the church. I commented that had I known she wanted coffee for the ride, I could have had one of my coworkers go before the end of mass and have it ready for our ride. That's when Eileen told me, "Now, Kevin, we will go to Dunkin Donuts for coffee like we always have in the past." That's when I knew that we would stop for coffee.

When I found a spot and parked, she tried to hand me a ten, but I insisted that I always bought coffee, and we would not break tradition on that one. I returned with three coffees, all with cream and sugar like I always did, and we then hit the highway for Boston.

As I drove, I thought, "Oh God, someone will see the casket in the back, the nameplates in the hearse's window, and call the funeral home to complain," which they didn't. Although, if they had, the correct response would have been "Well, the lady who is the sister of the deceased is in the front passenger seat and is also paying the bill. If she wants coffee, she gets coffee!"

Once to the cemetery, I assembled the pallbearers, and we placed the casket onto the grave. Eileen instructed me to put Mary's coffee beside the casket. I did. She then had me come sit beside her and held my hand as the priest performed the committal service.

As we returned to the hearse and Eileen said goodbye to her nieces and nephews, she told me we would stop for a late afternoon lunch at one of their favorite restaurants, which we did. As we enjoyed our lunch, she thanked me for being with her that day and for all that I had done to make Mary's funeral proper and fitting. I said that it was my honor; We toasted Mary and reveled in stories from the years since we had known each other and from their youth.

It was three years later that I went through that scenario again. Eileen had fallen ill and was not getting any better. It was in the Fall that I received the notification from the hospital that she had died, and I reached out to the one niece she was closest to. I made the arrangements for her funeral mass and the burial in Boston. I penned the obituary for the newspaper, and I followed through on everything, just as she had planned it.

As I departed the church, I made my way to the Dunkin Donuts. Again, I parked and went inside for two with cream and sugar. Again, I grew nervous about if someone saw the casket and complained. It was neither professional nor ethical to park a hearse with a casket in the back in plain sight and go in for food or coffee, but if you knew Eileen, you knew we would not break tradition.

As I drove, I recalled the first day that I met Mary and Eileen. I reminisced our conversations and all the times that we shared coffee, cookies and laughter. I missed Mary, and I would primarily miss Eileen! She was undoubtedly one of a kind.

Once at the gravesite, the pallbearers placed the casket; I removed the flowers from the hearse, and I set Eileen's coffee beside the casket. As the priest recited the committal prayers, I looked up and knew Eileen was smiling down on us all.

On my way back to the Cape, I stopped at the restaurant that was a favorite of Mary and Eileen. I had a quick bite to eat, and I probably garnered some strange looks as I toasted to my two friends.

I miss those days. Life was a little easier. The World was not in such a rush to get somewhere, and there was always time for coffee, time for cookies, and a time for laughter.

Another story I look back on and laugh revolves around a little old elderly lady whom I had the pleasure of working with to bury her husband. She was a lovely lady whose husband had pre-deceased her. I met with her and her son, who was an attorney in the Boston area. They selected the arrangements they wanted. Straightforward services, a very modest/middle of the road casket, and everything the same day.

The funeral was an intimate setting of family and close friends. They did not have a large, extended family as some. She purchased two graves at the local municipal cemetery, and she relied on life insurance to pay for the balance.

About six months later, she called the funeral home asking for myself. She wanted to make an appointment to come in and take care of her prearrangements. She arrived, and we chatted for a bit. I had pulled her husband's record, and we discussed her ideas for her arrangements.

She wanted everything to be the same, except she wanted a more feminine casket.

After showing her other available caskets and staying within the same cost range as his, we completed everything. We handled the payment; I made two copies for her and her son, as I always prefer to do. It always makes sense for someone else in the family to have a copy of such important papers. We chatted for a while longer, and I walked her out to her car.

Two days later, I walked in from finishing a funeral and had a missed call from a gentleman. It was a Boston area code. I tried to place the name. Then I remembered it was the last name of the lady I made pre-arrangements on, two days prior. It must be her son, I thought.

After a few minutes of getting settled, and after I had pulled her file, I returned his call. After his receptionist answered and transferred my call to him, he asked if his mother had come in and made her arrangements. I stated that she did, and I also made a copy for him as I usually do. He then became irate. "How could I do that? How could I take advantage of his mother? How much did she spend? He knows what the laws are and how long she has to cancel those prearrangements. I want answers and I want them now."

Once I got him to stop so I could get a word in and to settle down, I asked him what his fax number was. He gave me the number. I stated that I would fax copies of which we could go over together. I also informed him I would call him back in five minutes so we could go over said copies.

After confirming receipt of the fax, I waited a few minutes. I called the son, and we went over all the details and the amount of the transaction. He read over everything and responded, "Well, that can't be right." He asked me about the amount of which I confirmed, even noting the copy of her check and receipt that I attached. He still seemed confused. I asked him what was unclear. Why would he question what I had sent?

He then stated that his mother had told him she had handled her own arrangements; she had paid for everything and that the casket she selected was Top Shelf. I then sat and thought. I thought more.

After several seconds, I began to laugh. As I laughed, the son became upset and started asking me why I was laughing. After I could compose myself, I informed him yes; the casket was Top Shelf. It was on the top shelf of a three-tiered display rack in our selection room.

A common term in the New England area, and some other regions, is Top Shelf, meaning the Best of the Best. So yes, maybe in her eyes, the casket she had selected, which she referred to as a lovely lavender, was top shelf. But, in all actuality, it was between $1500–1600 dollars and what most would consider the middle of the road.

After clearing up the confusion, he apologized about misinterpreting what he assumed his mother was conveying to him. He said he remembered how well he and his mother were treated when planning for his father and thought it was a misunderstanding. But he wanted to call and make sure. We conversed for a few more minutes, laughing about the terminology and finishing our conversation.

16.

It was always nice to see family members showing up for a visitation and friends attending showing support for the family. I always preferred working a visitation as opposed to a funeral service. Still less formal and yet more of a social event.

And even as homey as some funeral homes can seem, I often wondered what went through people's minds sometimes. Many times I would see a young family come in and visit with the family. After a while, they would plop their toddler down on the carpet to crawl around on the floor. They are putting their hands into their mouths. And I would shudder at the thought. In my mind, I am saying, "My God! If you saw what happens in the embalming room, what gets splashed on the floor and that we walk through and then walk out here. You would think twice about placing that baby down onto that carpet."

Just like every instance when a family says, "We would like the clothing back after the visitation and funeral." My response is then, "No. We have no way to launder it, and it would pose a health hazard if we were to return it. You are more than welcome to give us clothing for your loved one to wear, that is less of sentimental value."

One day at a visitation, I had the son of a deceased gentleman tell me he wanted his father's jacket back after the services. It was a member's jacket for the local yacht club that the gentleman belonged to for years. I informed him we don't return the clothing. He even said, "Well, what's keeping me from going up there and taking it off myself and taking it home?" My response was, "I don't think I would advise that." His eyes widened as if he thought I was challenging him. And I may have if we weren't in the funeral home.

I went into even more detail: "Death is not as clean and sanitary as people think. The minute life ceases, you decompose. The body continues to urinate, defecate. The decomposition is only slowed by the embalming process. Upon putting on that jacket after it's worn by a deceased person and once that embalming fluid transfers from the clothing to your skin, I am sure that the carcinogens would also provide a rather nasty rash. Not to mention, you would have to take it to a tailor to have the back re-sewn, where we had to cut it to get it on him." That ended the discussion about the jacket.

Another story that I always tell involves a funeral home that closed years ago in the panhandle of Florida. A gentleman whom I met when I planned his father's funeral some time ago had some experience in the funeral business. His dad worked part-time years ago, and he had some experience in the embalming room.

Back when that property was closed and sold, the new owner sold what they could, for what they could get. Then they concentrated on renovating the building for resale. Some said items made it to thrift and second-hand shops.

One day that young man went to a buddy's house and had been told that they were having a crawfish boil and a crab boil. The entire family was there. They had tons of food and beer, to come on over and partake and visit with the family. I think they were celebrating a graduation or something.

Upon arrival, he greeted his friend, grabbed a beer, and made his way around greeting and visiting with the family. As they made their way out back where the food was, his friend was describing what an incredible find he made at the local thrift store. He had gained a large stainless steel table that had a gutter like a rim around the perimeter. You could adjust one end lower than the other, and the lower end had a hole and a hook. You could easily hang a bucket from the hook below the hole which they did. He exclaimed how it made an exceptional Crawfish Table, which could catch all the shells and juice, and you empty the bucket every so often.

With his curiosity heightened, they make their way over to where this new, modern marvel is. And, as he stated, there in the middle of the table, was a crawfish boil, complete with crawfish, corn, potatoes, and sausage. As the host graciously invited him to grab a plate and dig in, he respectfully declined and said: "No, thank you." The host then said, "What, you don't like crawfish?" And he replied, "No, I love crawfish! However, I don't enjoy eating it off an embalming table!"

 I wished I could have seen the look on their faces. He said people were spitting food onto the ground and chugging their beverages to cleanse their palates. Some of those folks were sipping on homemade corn liquor and drank that down, purely for the sterilization factor.

I laugh like Hell when I think of that story. I don't think there is any amount of bleach that they could clean that table with to make it possible that I could eat off of it.

Grief affects everyone differently. Some people ignore it, and some deal with it the best that they can. Some deal with it in healthy ways, and some in a not so healthy manner. Grief can drive folks towards depression and to not be cognitive of their own well-being, diet, etc. Unhealthy habits, substance abuse and other addictions, can make their way into anyone's life, based on the loneliness and sadness..

Years ago, I started a grief support group at one of the funeral homes that I managed. I worked it out to where the funeral home paid an honorarium to the local hospice chaplain that covered his time for the one-hour meeting, once a month and the workbooks we copied and printed for all that attended. The support group was a little slow to get going, but when it did, it took right off.

We quickly grew from just a few participants to well over 15 - 20 at one point. Men were the hardest to convince to attend, as they did not think they needed it. But once they attended, almost all returned. From the group, we had several clicks of women that would gather and walk at the local mall, some of which would meet for lunch and shopping outings and some men for fishing outings. It felt good to help these folks see past their grief and re-invest themselves back into living.

We had attendees that were spouses, parents, children, siblings, and even grandchildren. These were people who needed some guidance or a way to talk past their experience with grief. It was also an excellent means to offer an aftercare program, which is also a unique opportunity for any funeral home.

I also worked with a local humane society at the inception of a foster program for several of the members to become a foster home for displaced pets. The humane society was apprehensive at first, but it worked out as a win for everyone. Many people who have lost a loved one and are suffering through grief lose that drive to get up and motivated in the morning. They had to get up and get their day started because they had someone relying on them for care and help. With that person gone, they sometimes lose that drive.

With the addition of a pet to the household, it again gives them that sense that someone depends on them for care. And many times a companion, to spend time with and make life a little more manageable. I will admit that the humane society was apprehensive about coming on board, and I went out on a limb to convince them it was good for everyone involved. But I can understand their concern for the animal should things not work out.

I used to stop by and perform home visits and check up on those that I paired with a pet. I had a curriculum I had to follow to make sure all was well, and I had to answer to the folks at the adoption institute. I often brought stuffed toys and dog food with me on said visits, but I wanted to make sure this worked out and that these folks could afford that added expense, and care. It's hard enough to take care of an older individual on a fixed income. You throw the added expense of a pet into the mix and that adds up. I spent a few bucks on a vet bill here and there, but I knew I was doing the right thing and deep down I was happy to do so.

It felt good to be a funeral director; it felt terrific to see the smile on these people's faces and it was a pleasure to get any pet out of the shelter and feel loved again.

18.

Mistakes, we've all made a few. And hopefully, we learn from them as we go. I know I have, and I have always taken the time to double-check afterward so I don't make the same one again.

I will now rattle off more memorable ones. Some are mine, some are others, but I learned from them all.

I once went to the hospital almost thirty years ago as an apprentice to make a removal. I signed out with security and checked the tag on the outside of the body bag. I returned to the funeral home and went to place the person into the cooler. I signed that person into the log, and I checked the toe tag. The name on the toe tag did not match the name on the outside of the bag. I had to go back to the hospital and explain how I picked up the wrong body. Someone had mis-marked the outside of the bag differently from the name of the decedent. That was when I learned always to check all the tags.

The embalmers and funeral directors will relate to this. Aspiration is part of the embalming procedure. It comprises inserting a long 24-inch tube with a pointy end called a trocar into the body near the belly button. The purpose of aspiration is to remove the blood and other body fluids from the thoracic and abdominal cavities. This procedure ensures that you are drying out the said area, and you will later inject formaldehyde to treat and to firm said area.

When performing aspiration, as part of the embalming procedure, you always take hold of the diverter and give it a quick 180-degree turn every 2-5 minutes. The diverter is the lever on the side of the hydro aspirator, which is a plumbing fixture hooked up to a water line. With the diverter in one direction, the aspirator sprays water. In the other direction, it performs suction. It is essential to give it that twist of the lever every few minutes to prevent it from backing up. Not to sound gross, but tissue will accumulate, causing it to back up and go from suction to spraying. By twisting said lever, you are clearing out any tissue that could cause a back-up.

Back in the '80s, as an apprentice, I assisted on an embalming. The embalmer said, OK, you have it from here. You finish the aspiration. Once you have done that, you inject the cavity fluid, cover it with cotton, and pose the hands back in their normal folded position. I thought, no problem, I've got this. And I did. It was going well and so easy until about 1o minutes after he left when I heard that dreadful God awful sound.

Things went from the typical suction sound to a very distinct, quieter sound. I turned and looked at the clear tubing coming from the aspirator to the body on the table. The usual red fluid and color that left the body, going down the drain, were quickly reversing and going back into the point of aspiration. As I looked and saw that the liquid was now clear and that water was being injected back into the person, I freaked out. I jumped and overreacted. Instead of twisting the diverter, or the logical process of turning off the water faucet, I quickly pulled the trocar out.

Huge mistake! When I did what I thought was the right thing to do, that shit went everywhere! Oh, God I yelled! Amongst other expletives. I was so disgusted. That red, bloody fluid went all over me, the person I was embalming, every nook, and cranny of the room and behind every piece of furniture in the embalming room.

The bad part of the situation was not the extra labor and cleaning. That was a learning experience and part of life. Shit happens, and you roll with the punches. The bad part of the ordeal was that this person's casket was nearby and opened. It was a lovely 18 gauge metal protective casket that had a powder blue interior. A powder blue interior, now speckled with red bodily fluids! And I was beside myself. Before I cleaned anything else, I addressed the casket situation. I used everything I could think of to remove those stains. I tried cold water, soap and water, a cleaning solvent, and even lighter fluid. Everything that I had ever heard of that might work.

The direct hit from this blood cannon and its red peppered shrapnel took place at about 9 PM. After I scrubbed every inch of the prep room and tried to clean the casket, it was about 2 AM when I finally locked up and entered my car to go home.

The next day I thought for sure I would be on the unemployment line when I explained my mistake and the dilemma with the casket. As I entered my boss's office and told him I needed to tell him something, he sat down. I confessed my mishap with the latter part of the embalming procedure, and his eyes got real big. He appeared to get agitated, and then he became understanding. He said it happened before, and he then called the local York Casket distributor to see if we could get a replacement interior and what the cost would be.

It worked out as we had time to correct my mishap. And, as time went on, I learned not to let that happen again. You always give the diverter a quick 180-degree twist, every 2-5 minutes to break any buildup of tissue, fat or fascia that may have built up inside. It works, and many people look at me funny when I say it, but it will prevent a disaster! And, to this day, I learned not to open the casket or remove its protective plastic covering until you are ready to place its intended occupant inside.

Years ago, back in Worcester, as an apprentice, I was a little too enthusiastic in trying to detail my employer's Cadillac Fleetwood one day for a funeral. It was just two little old ladies that would follow the hearse and no need for a limousine, so my boss said he would drive them and that I should detail his car to make it presentable for the funeral. I did so the afternoon prior before I had to drive to Classes.

The next morning, we had the viewing at the funeral home. After calling the car list, and everyone adjourned to their vehicles. We placed the casket into the hearse, the flowers into the flower car, and we processed to the church. Once the casket was in the church and in place in front of the altar, we exited. I was about to make the coffee and donut run for everyone when my boss pulled me aside and said,

"Hey. When you were cleaning my car for the funeral, did you put anything on the seats?"

I thought for a moment, and then I remarked, "Just Armor All. I thought it would make the seats nice and shiny." His eyes got real big, and then he said, "Yeah. We probably need not do that anymore. That backseat is so slippery, every time I took a left or right, those two ladies would slide to the opposite end of the backseat. I'm surprised neither one broke a hip. Once they slammed into the door so hard I thought it had come open and they were on the street. They finally had to put their seatbelts on to hold them into place."

I felt terrible afterward, but later I laughed at how that must have looked. Thank God it hurt no one, but I can imagine the look on his face, being upfront, and not knowing what was going on.

I once listed a woman's usual occupation as a Hoemaker instead of a Homemaker on a death certificate. I caught my mistake when I was standing at the vital statistics window filing the document. It took a lot of begging, pleading, and sad eyes on my part to convince the town clerk to let me take it back to the funeral home and correct my typo. Once in her hand, an affidavit should be filed, taking weeks, and a monetary amount to fix the said error. She took pity on me and let me correct it after convincing her that the woman's daughter would probably beat my ass when and if she read the error.

I once embalmed and prepared a woman for her visitation and funeral. I completed her makeup, dressed, and placed her into her casket. I went to great detail to make sure everything was just right. I was standing at the front door, waiting for the director to check on the family. I felt good when they said, "Mama looks so beautiful. She looks years younger and like she is resting." What I didn't expect to hear was, "There is only one problem, her dress is on backwards." it horrified me I could make such a stupid mistake. After that error, I came up with the rhyme that I say when dressing a female. I always say, "Don't be a hack, make sure the tag is in the back."

I once made a home removal and forgot to replace a new pouch on the stretcher that we customarily place the body in when doing so. It was a house with tight turns and corners. We had to stand the cot on end to maneuver our way out of the residence. After placing the stretcher into the vehicle, I made my way back into the home to work out an appointment time to meet with the family. That's when I noticed the trail of urine drops that followed us out to our vehicle. I never forgot to replenish the pouch on the stretcher again.

We once picked up a man that had died at home on his couch in a seated position. The wife stated that she wanted his wallet removed and given to her before moving him. Just as I noticed a slight bit of purge on the corner of his mouth, the new apprentice commenced to roll him forward to reach in his pocket and remove the wallet. As word, no could not leave my mouth soon enough; the gentleman leaked purge all down his chin, clothing, all over the white couch and all over the white carpet. That's when I learned a valuable lesson. If you are moving an individual and the casket or stretcher is to open again for viewing, you always keep the head elevated!

You always check the names on the flowers before setting them up for a visitation or placing them into a vehicle to go to a funeral. I was bitten in the ass once, and I vowed I would never have to pay for flowers again after that mistake.

Always examine a decedent before you make any promises to a family. Expectations about the ability to view and presentation can have different meanings for different people. Never take someone else's opinion about the said condition of a decedent.

When making a late-night removal at a nursing home, always recite the room number and corresponding bed back to the nurse at the nurses' station. I once had a nurse tell me Room 130, Bed A, at 3:00 AM. My partner and I roll into Room 130 and pull the curtain back at Bed A.

As we reached under to pull the gentleman over onto the stretcher, he got startled and jumped, as did the two of us. He yelled, "Get off of me, you son of a Bitch!" As I tried to pull my head back, he threw a right that connected with the left side of my jaw. I will have to say this. That man could throw a punch. I've caught a few punches over the years, and that one caught me off guard. It's one thing to see it coming and to clench your teeth and prepare for it, as to not chip a tooth when being hit with an open mouth. But my mouth was open. I didn't have time to clench, and I only bit my tongue. But it quit bleeding by the time we got back to the funeral home.

When he calmed down and asked what we were doing, I told him to go back to sleep. We are doing bed checks to make sure everyone is

OK. We pulled the curtain and proceeded to Bed B. At his point, I'm thinking Jesus! What the Hell just happened. That nurse gave us the wrong bed. Hell, we could even be in the wrong room for all I know! At Bed B, I gave the gentleman a few soft pokes to the shoulder to make sure we were at the correct bed. I even opened the drawer and spotted some belongings that had his name on them, matching the name they had given us from the answering service.

I stopped and corrected the nurse which bed she had given us. She apologized. I told her to please be more mindful about the info she is passing on. I know we all get busy, and we all make mistakes, but it makes a difference, and I could have easily given that poor man a heart attack! Not to mention the fact that he almost gave me one. As I left, I bid her farewell and told her to have a good night. I now needed to go so I could get a clean change of underwear. She apologized again, but laughed at the underwear comment.

 As my buddy, Greg would say, when you are working a visitation and talking to a lady with one of those handheld oxygen machines. If it makes a funny noise, and she makes odd faces, look down and make sure you are not standing on the line leading upwards to her face.

Always make sure you check the clothing and name on said clothing that you are about to place on the decedent, before their service. This too bit me on the ass once, years ago. We were able to catch the mistake and make the correction. And, if one of your coworkers is working with you in the embalming room, helping you dress an individual, make sure it is not his suit jacket that you are cutting up the back. Luckily, the company replaced his coat.

When parking and lining up cars for a funeral procession, always remove the keys from inside the vehicle or leave a window cracked. As an apprentice, I once had a car that automatically locked with the keys in the ignition and alarm armed. It's not fun when your boss has to spring for a locksmith.

In this modern-day technology, cell phones can be a good thing and a bad thing. I once had a priest refer to a deceased gentleman by the wrong name. I caught said mistake, as I am sure the family did. Instead of getting up and making that awkward walk to the altar from the front pew to correct him, I quickly pulled out my phone and texted one of my coworkers. He ran around to the side entrance of the church, scrawled the correct name on a large piece of cardboard and held it up from the side of the altar.

He was out of sight of everyone except the organist, soloist, and myself. Suddenly, you hear a loud Pssssstttt. The priest looks in his direction, squints to read the large sign, and then yells out the correct name. It was all the three of us could do, not to break out in hysterics! He apologized to the family afterward. The family remarked about what a jokester Dad was and that he would have laughed immensely at it.

Years ago, as an apprentice, one of the local medical examiners asked me to draw blood from a deceased gentleman. They had supplied us with a kit to do so. I removed the syringe and attached the needle and removed the top from the two small bottles that I was to fill and label. With my fingers, I located a space between two ribs and inserted the needle. I tried several times to withdraw blood from all four chambers of the heart. I had no success. I repeatedly tried and still could not remove a sample.

I had already raised the carotid and jugular and inserted the cannula to begin the embalming process. I thought, no problem. I'll place the needle into the jugular and pull some from there. I did so, the medical examiner picked it up and left later that day. Several weeks later, I received a call from the same ME. The conversation began with "Hey, remember Mr. Smith, who I asked that you to pull a blood sample from back a few weeks ago?" I responded, "Yes." He replied, "How did you acquire that sample?"

When I explained to him the difficulty that I had to get a sample, his reply was, "Yeah, never do that again. I just got off of the phone with his family, and it highly upset them that I put ethanol abuse on the death certificate when the man hasn't touched alcohol in his entire life."

I inadvertently must have gotten a few trace amounts of embalming fluid in the sample I had taken.

Always take the time to proofread an obituary. Always tell anyone that the deadline for the newspaper is an hour earlier than it is. You still need that extra hour to prepare before sending it to the press, and you will always have that one person who wants to send it to you five minutes before the deadline.

The same goes for the needed things for the funeral. I always move the time up for requested items such as clothing, pictures, 24 hours before we require them. There is still that person who waits until the last moment to bring things in, and no one needs that stress.

As callous as it sounds, always secure payment before scheduling a funeral, placing an obituary, or committing to a date or time. Funeral homes need to work with families in certain instances on payment, and most directors hate to be that way, but there are the bad apples that have made it this way.

Years ago, I helped the family of a young man who had died as the result of a robbery and someone stealing his unlawful substances. I met with the family, made the arrangements, and scheduled everything as they assured me they had an account set up at the bank to cover the costs. They did not come to the funeral home the day before the funeral and pay as they claimed they would. I stressed the fact that I needed payment in hand at the Church on the day of the funeral. They agreed.

The next day, we set up at the church for the funeral. The family arrived, they went into grieving mode, and I noticed that the one aunt of the deceased young man was absent. I finally pulled the father aside and addressed the payment issue. He then told me that the aunt who was spearheading the financial part of everything had fled with the money. I told him I was sorry to hear that, but I needed that money to pay the cemetery, casket, and vault companies.

After a few minutes of calming down and thought, I called the cemetery and asked them if we could cover the grave for 24 hours, without incurring a second opening of the grave fee. They agreed. I then returned to the father, and I assured him we would have the funeral, and the procession to the cemetery, and committal service. After everyone's departure, we would bring the casket back to the funeral home, and he had twenty-four hours to work out the payment issue. I would make nothing seem out of the ordinary for people to suspect that something was not right. And, if I were to get fired over the issue, he would have to deal with someone else, who may not be as understanding as myself.

Later that day, I received a call from his employer. They were sending a distribution from the father's retirement plan. A loan of which he had to repay. He asked if I would then do the burial the next day. I agreed under the terms they fax me a copy of the check and the overnight envelope. That way, I knew the money was coming.

I didn't sleep too well that night. I felt awful about having to be put in that position, but I learned a valuable lesson. Since that day, I have always completed payment before scheduling or publicizing the date or time of a funeral. Some people may think that is a harsh thing to say or do, but trust me. Once you're placed in that position, you never want to be put there again. Many smaller, family-owned funeral homes would have to close their doors if they had to rely on the honor system. And, there are those that would not think twice about doing that to any small businessman or businesswoman.

Yeah, we all make mistakes. But it's up to us to learn from them to grow to become a better person.

I couldn't imagine doing anything that I disliked. For me, I enjoyed being a funeral director. I enjoyed hearing the stories about the person who had passed. I enjoyed embalming. I enjoyed knowing that I could do my best to make it so that their family could view them one last time. I enjoyed that I could allow the family an opportunity to have that closure. I cared about being true to myself, the family of which I served and the dignity that their loved one deserved.

Being a funeral director also placed me in the right place at the right time to take advantage of certain opportunities that I might have otherwise missed. I've handled funeral arrangements for several famous actors, celebrities and family members of celebrities, both here in Florida and back on Cape Cod.

It has given me the opportunity to work on several notable forensic cases, which included the reinvestigation of the Boston Strangler case in 2001. In doing so, I had an appearance on television shows 20/20 and 48 Hours and being mentioned in the updated chapters of The Boston Stranglers by Susan Kelly.

I've had the opportunities to work alongside and under Professor James E. Starrs of George Washington University, Forensic Scientist Dr. Henry Lee and Forensic Pathologist Dr. Michael Baden, all whom I had idolized for years in their careers and work. Having studied and read many volumes of each of their case studies and work, I leaped at the opportunity to aid and study under each of them.

I also landed a film role in the motion picture Finding Her Way Home, back in 2011. The writer was looking for a funeral home to film several scenes in. She was not only happy to find a location to shoot in, but I also worked out the ability of filming to occur at the cemetery, equipment loaned from the local vault company and a procession with escorts from the local police department. All with their mention at the end of the film and in credits, as agreed. I even landed the role of a Catholic Priest. Of which those that know me hysterically laugh, when I tell them.

Yeah, being a funeral director has been good to me over the years. I wouldn't trade it for the world, but it can be work. It isn't always a glamorous role as we see on TV, and it's not a career suited for everyone. You pull your dues. You go out at all hours of the night to pick someone up. Sometimes you get yelled at and treated like crap by people you don't even know who have suffered a loss and are looking to take it out on someone. You make mistakes; you learn from them and you forge ahead.

You damage suits and clothing. You spend Christmas and many other holidays away from your family because death knows no holiday or schedule. You catch the stink eye from your daughter because you're 15 minutes late to her school play, of which you assured her you would be on time for. And you were late because you had finished the arrangements conference, but that one member of the family wouldn't stop talking held you up. You do it. You do it with a smile and sometimes for meager pay. But you do it because deep down; It feels good to make a difference.

And my words of advice to anyone that wishes to become a funeral director, it's a rewarding job, one that you can fall in love with and feel good about your purpose in life.

There are good days, there will be bad days and long days. But what you need to understand is that it's not all Cadillacs, suits and roses.

I've spent countless hours walking cemeteries. Local cemeteries, veteran's affairs cemeteries and little old country cemeteries. I have always found it fascinating to read the headstones. I have always looked at the dates, ages and personal inscriptions. Some memorialization cut into the granite or marble tell a story of the person there. Sometimes it is the tears that flow that tell the story. Stories of people who have impacted our lives, those that we had the pleasure and opportunity to know, work with, or be related. Stories that people will continue to tell at parties, gatherings and during the holidays.

Many times I have sat at the table meeting with a family. Listening to their stories. Taking notes and information that the family wished to be in the obituary. And often I have sat there and thought "Man, I wished I could have sat and talked with this guy. He sounds like one Hell of a Man." Stories of hurdles and personal challenges that person had to encounter during life. Sacrifices made to meet the needs and take care of his family. Stories of challenges that the person met for their country. I have read somber obituaries, Prolific obituaries, and encountered people who choose not to have an obituary. And I have read obituaries of "She may have been a wee petite little lady, but she wouldn't hesitate to tell you where the Bear goes to do his business in the Woods type of lady."

Over time, I have always encouraged a family to gather pictures for a collage for display at the visitation/funeral or even nowadays, for the video presentation. It's not only a nice display, but it's also therapeutic for the family When they look through the pictures to choose ones for the presentation, they talk, laugh, cry and that creates a healing time of which they may not have achieved any other way. I have often made just that comment and many people have acknowledged that it helped.

In this age of everyone staring into their cell phones and fixated on something other than spending time together as a family, it's one of the few things that will bring people closer. The old saying of "We only see each other at weddings and funerals" is very true. Wakes and funerals used to be an event that occurred over several days. Then it transpired to two days with the wake the night before the funeral. Now, we are seeing people that want to do it all in one day.

Not only are things more recently about convenience, people are looking for convenience and savings. In this day of bargain outlets and price advertising, funeral homes have to follow suit. As tradition changes, so do the way people do things. More and more, I am hearing "Just cremate me and have a Big Party." And that's what people are doing.

People are more inclined to have a memorial service without the body present and a reception with food and beverages after. Some of those that still hold religion as a meaningful part of their lives will have that service at the church and then a reception afterwards. Nowadays you are having fewer services in the church than you did years ago. I think a lot of it is formality. Most of the older generation want a more formal ceremony in the church or at the funeral home, structured with a priest or pastor and a service. Most of the younger generation is looking for that less formal route, with a memorial service and party after.

Whichever route you prefer, religious, non-religious, formal or informal, the important thing is that you have some service. The service is for the living and closure for those that survive to grieve and mourn the loss. It can be as formal or as informal as the family wishes. It should be much like the life of the person it is for. We should fill it with tears, laughter, stories, love and above anything else, a time to bring people together. There is too much BS in this world. There is too much stubbornness, too much hatred and too many people in a hurry. In a hurry for what? We're all going to die. It's a part of life.

The important thing to remember is that everyone's life tells a story. It's up to you to make it an interesting one.

A life that is loved, cherished, mourned, revelled and celebrated.